LEGENDS OF EARLY ROME

LEGENDS OF EARLY ROME

Authentic Latin Prose for the Beginning Student

Brian Beyer

Yale

UNIVERSITY PRESS

New Haven and London

Yale University Press books may be
purchased in quantity for educational,
business, or promotional use. For
information, please e-mail sales.press@
yale.edu (U.S. office) or sales@yaleup
.co.uk (U.K. office).

Editor: Tim Shea
Publishing Assistant: Ashley E. Lago
Manuscript Editor: Juliana Froggatt
Production Editor: Ann-Marie Imbornoni
Production Controller: Katie Golden

Maps by Bill Nelson.

Set in Scala type by Integrated Publishing
Solutions.
Printed in the United States of America.

Library of Congress Control Number:
2015936438
ISBN: 978-0-300-16543-2 (pbk. : alk.
paper)

A catalogue record for this book is
available from the British Library.

This paper meets the requirements of
ANSI/NISO Z39.48-1992 (Permanence
of Paper).

10 9 8 7 6 5 4 3 2 1

It is the privilege of antiquity to mingle divine things with human, and so to add dignity to the beginnings of cities; and if any people ought to be allowed to consecrate their origins and refer them to a divine source, so great is the military glory of the Roman People that when they profess that their Father and the Father of their Founder was none other than Mars, the nations of the earth may well submit to this also with as good a grace as they submit to Rome's dominion.

—Livy, *Ab urbe condita* I, preface

CONTENTS

PREFACE

Why Eutropius?

Since the publication of *War with Hannibal* in 2009 I have heard from students, teachers, and independent learners alike how helpful Eutropius has been in making the transition from a Latin textbook to reading real Latin literature. Even purportedly easy authors like Caesar and Nepos are in reality too difficult without adequate preparation. Eutropius's vocabulary, style, and syntax provide an ideal foundation for reading authors such as these. He writes in good, standard classical Latin and uses nearly all of the most common and important grammatical constructions. His vocabulary, however, is quite simple, and his sentences are not overly long or complex. This gives students the opportunity to develop their skill and confidence in reading extended Latin prose, without getting lost in a morass of subordination or arcane vocabulary.

This new volume of Eutropius, then, is meant to contribute to the options available to those who wish to make a more seamless transition to Caesar or a similar author, while still using authentic Latin literature. It may be used on its own or in conjunction with *War with Hannibal* (the two volumes together include two complete books, approximately three thousand words, of Eutropius's *Breviarium ab urbe condita*).

Book I of the *Breviarium* covers a period of Roman history that should have wide appeal to both high school and college instructors: from the founding of the city in 753 BCE to the sack of Rome by the Gauls in 390 BCE. Eutropius's narrative is presented without any adaptations or omissions (except for the deletion of a single clause in the first sentence of chapter I and a short personal interjection addressed to the emperor Valens in chapter XII). Since the main source for Eutropius's abbreviation of Roman history was an Epitome of Livy, generous passages in English from Livy supplement the Latin text, adding color and detail to Eutropius's succinct account. Historical notes—set off in boxes for easy reference— are provided in the Commentary, with special attention to questions of historicity.

As with *War with Hannibal*, it typically takes three to four weeks to read this text in its entirety at the college level. Thus it may be used as the "payoff" immediately after finishing an elementary textbook, or as an opportunity for review and reinforcement at the beginning of year two. At the high school level, either alone or in conjunction with *War with Hannibal*, the text provides an excellent foundation for the Caesar portions of the AP curriculum.

Format of This Edition

Since this text is meant to be a student's first encounter with continuous Latin prose, the amount of translation help given is quite liberal. It comes in a number of forms: The most basic glosses—the ones most readers will need to "get" the Latin—are beneath the text, where they are easily accessible. More in-depth translation help, formal analyses of the grammar and syntax, and historical notes are placed in the Commentary in the back of the book. This allows for an ample running commentary while leaving the simple glosses unencumbered.

The Commentary need not be read in its entirety but may be referred to on an as-needed basis. As such, basic translation help and identification of perfect participles, subjunctives, and the like are not phased out over the course of the notes. More lengthy discussions of grammar and syntax (e.g., regarding ablatives absolute and purpose clauses) take place only at the first occurrence of the element in question. Readers who would like to refer to these sections may easily do so by means of the Index of Selected Grammatical Constructions.

All grammatical principles in the Commentary are cross-referenced to *Cambridge Latin Course: Unit 3*, 4th Edition (New York: Cambridge University Press, 2002), *Ecce Romani II*, 4th Edition (Upper Saddle River, NJ: Prentice Hall, 2009), *Jenney's Second Year Latin* (Upper Saddle River, NJ: Prentice Hall, 1990), *Latin: An Intensive Course* (Berkeley: University of California Press, 1977), *Latin for Americans*, Level 2 (New York: Glencoe/McGraw-Hill, 2004), *Latin for the New Millennium*, Level 2 (Mundelein, IL: Bolchazy-Carducci, 2009), *Learn to Read Latin* (New Haven: Yale University Press, 2003), *Oxford Latin Course, Part III*, 2nd Edition (New York: Oxford University Press, 1997), *Wheelock's Latin*, 7th Edition, Revised (New York: Harper Collins, 2011), and *Allen and Greenough's New Latin Grammar* (Boston: Ginn, 1903). This last is available online from the Perseus Digital Library at www.perseus.tufts.edu.

A section with only the bare Latin text has been included for use during classroom translation. Not having the notes under the student's eye in the classroom ensures that the glosses are not used as a crutch and that grammatical concepts have been thoroughly learned. The inclusion of the bare text as a separate section allows the "user-friendly" bottom-of-the-page glosses to be preserved in the Text and Notes section for the student's initial contact with the text.

The Appendices include maps of Rome and Latium in the fifth century BCE, and a bibliography lists those texts, commentaries, and translations of Eutropius most relevant to students. An Index of Selected Grammatical Constructions is included so that teachers may locate illustrative examples of particular constructions.

Vocabulary

The Vocabulary has been compiled specifically for Book I of Eutropius's *Breviarium*. The entries have been adapted in part from Lewis and Short's *Latin Dictionary* (New York: Harper and Brothers, 1897) and other standard lexica.

The Vocabulary also contains a number of features helpful to the beginning student: all forms whose dictionary entry might not be immediately recognized (e.g., irregular perfects, perfect participles) are given individual entries pointing to the relevant lexical form; the elements of all compound words are shown in brackets; basic biographical information is included for all historical persons; entries are given for all forms of personal names that appear in the text (e.g., praenomen abbreviations); specific passages in Book I of the *Breviarium* are referenced where it seemed necessary to clarify the usage of a word. The inclusion of all inflected forms of a word after the dictionary entry—an innovative feature in a Latin commentary—allows the student to confirm that he or she has found the correct entry for a particular word.

Latin Text

The established texts of the major critical editions (see Bibliography) differ in only a few places in all of Book I of the *Breviarium*. The overarching principle used for establishing the Latin text of this edition was that of following the reading easiest for the beginning student. Because of the nature of the work, discussions of manuscript variants have been kept to the barest of minimums. Macrons, including hidden quantities, have been added to the entire text.

English Translations of Livy

The English translations of Livy's *Ab urbe condita* are from Livy, Volume I, Books 1–2, Loeb Classical Library Volume 114, translated by B. O. Foster, 1919; Livy, Volume II, Books 3–4, Loeb Classical Library Volume 133, translated by B. O. Foster, 1922.

Acknowledgments

There are many people to whom I owe a debt of gratitude for their help with this book. David Wright prepared a significant portion of the vocabulary and textbook cross-references. The ever-magnanimous Dale Grote and the eagle-eyed Allison Resnick read through the entire manuscript at an early stage and provided numerous, invaluable suggestions. My students at Montgomery High School suffered through the first drafts of this book and much improved it by their insights. Jason Barillaro, Ed DeHoratius, Rich Esswein, Anne Pearson, and Cary Riggs all kindly class-tested the book, and their students provided valuable feedback. I was extremely fortunate to have had Juliana Froggatt as the copy editor. Every page has been improved by her thoughtfulness and expertise. Finally, my wife Ruth, my son Benjamin, and my daughters Ariella and Eliana deserve much credit for putting up with my obsessiveness. *Super omnia, carissimi mihi sunt.*

INTRODUCTION

The aim of this book, like that of its predecessor, *War with Hannibal*, is simple: to make authentic, unadapted Latin prose accessible to the beginning student. It presents Book I of Eutropius's *Breviarium ab urbe condita*, which covers the period from the foundation of Rome in 753 BCE to the sack of the city by the Gauls in 390 BCE. Historical notes, providing context and addressing issues of historicity, can be found in the Commentary in the back of the book. For an excellent overview of this period, see the subentries "Origins of Rome" and "Early republic" under "Rome (History)" in the *Oxford Classical Dictionary*, 3rd edition (New York: Oxford University Press, 1996). For a more in-depth but highly accessible introduction to Rome's early history, see H. H. Scullard's *A History of the Roman World: 753 to 146 BC* (Abingdon, Oxfordshire: Routledge, 2012). For detailed coverage of historical and textual issues, see R. M. Ogilvie's *A Commentary on Livy, Books 1–5* (New York: Oxford University Press, 1965).

History of the *Breviarium ab urbe condita*

Eutropius wrote the *Breviarium ab urbe condita* in the latter half of the fourth century CE, during the reign of the emperors Valens and Valentinian I. The work, which consists of ten books, begins with the foundation of Rome in 753 BCE and ends with the death of the emperor Jovian in 364 CE. It was written for an aristocracy whose first language was often not Latin and who needed a succinct and readable history of Rome. It immediately became popular both in the West and, in translation, in the Byzantine world. Its popularity in the Middle Ages and the Renaissance is attested by the survival of more than eighty manuscripts, eleven from before the fifteenth century. The *Breviarium* even made it onto Petrarch's short list of favorite books (*Libri mei peculiares*) from 1333.

In the modern era, the *Breviarium* became a staple of the school curriculum in both the United States and Britain and was very often the first Latin text a student read. Many nineteenth-century educators regarded Caesar's *Commentarii de bello Gallico* as too difficult for use as a first Latin text and saw the *Breviarium* as an ideal "bridge text." The Report of the Committee of Twelve of the American Philological Association in 1899, for instance, suggests reading Eutropius just before Caesar. Similarly, Arrowsmith and Whicher's popular nineteenth-century reader includes three entire books of Eutropius before moving on to Caesar.

The *Breviarium* enjoyed a publication history from the eighteenth through the early twentieth century comparable to or greater than that of almost any other Latin text read in schools. In 1902, for example, there were no fewer than fourteen editions of the *Breviarium* in print in the United States and Britain. By contrast, in the same year there was a combined total of only ten editions of all works by Nepos in print. Furthermore, a number of editions of Eutropius enjoyed continuous reprints throughout the first half of the twentieth century. It was not until the late 1950s (a time when there was a new emphasis on introducing increasingly adult-age Latin students to Cicero and similar writers as soon as possible) that the last school edition of the *Breviarium* finally went out of print.

Life of Eutropius

Little is known about Eutropius. Apparently, he was from a wealthy but not senatorial family and was given a good education. He began a career as an imperial clerk under the emperor Constantine. We learn from a comment in the *Breviarium* that he served under the emperor Julian in his expedition against the Persians in 363 CE. Under the emperor Valens (to whom the *Breviarium* is dedicated), Eutropius was promoted to the senior imperial Secretariat (as *magister memoriae*). His survey of Roman history is his only work that has been preserved.

Eutropius's
Breviarium
ab urbe condita,
Liber primus

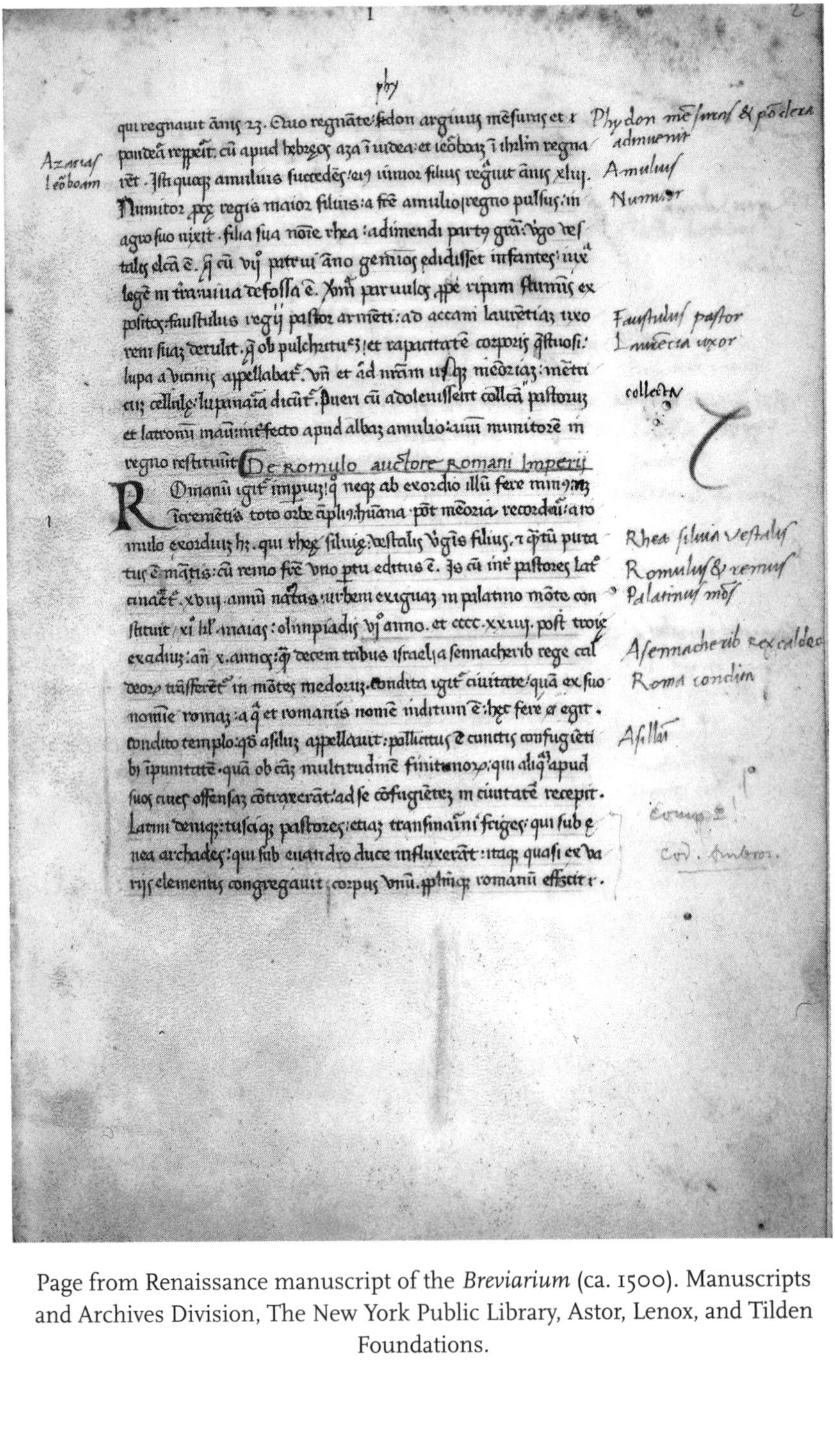

Page from Renaissance manuscript of the *Breviarium* (ca. 1500). Manuscripts and Archives Division, The New York Public Library, Astor, Lenox, and Tilden Foundations.

Text and Notes

Romulus and the foundation of Rome, 753–715 BCE

I. Rōmānum imperium ā Rōmulō exōrdium habet, quī Rēae Silviae, Vestālis virginis, filius et, quantum putātus est, Mārtis cum Remō frātre ūnō
partū ēditus est. Is, cum inter pāstōrēs latrōcinārētur, decem et octō annōs
nātus urbem exiguam in Palātīnō monte cōnstituit XI Kal. Maiās, Olympiadis sextae annō tertiō, post Trōiae excidium, ut quī plūrimum minimum-   5
que trādunt, annō trecentēsimō nōnāgēsimō quārtō.

1. **exōrdium habet** – *has its beginning* = *derives its origin.*
2. **ūnō partū** – *in one birth.*
3. **ēditus est** – *was brought forth.*
   cum . . . latrōcinārētur – *while he was leading the life of a bandit.*
   decem et octō annōs nātus – *having been born eighteen years* = *at eighteen
   years of age.*
4. **cōnstituit** – *established.*
   XI Kal. Maiās = *ante diem ūndecimum Kalendās Maiās, the eleventh day before the Kalends of May, i.e., April 21.*
   Olympiadis sextae annō tertiō – *in the third year of the sixth Olympiad, i.e.,
   753 BCE.*
5. **excidium** – *destruction.*
   ut quī plūrimum minimumque trādunt – *according to those who give the
   most and the least* = *according to the average of the earliest and latest dates.*
6. **trecentēsimō nōnāgēsimō quārtō** – *394th.*

ROMULUS AND REMUS

Since the brothers were twins, and respect for their age could not
determine between them, it was agreed that the gods who had
those places in their protection should choose by augury who
should give the new city its name, who should govern it when
built. . . . Thereupon each was saluted king by his own followers,
the one party laying claim to the honour from priority, the other
from the number of the birds. They then engaged in a battle of
words and, angry taunts leading to bloodshed, Remus was struck
down in the affray. The commoner story is that Remus leaped over
the new walls in mockery of his brother, whereupon Romulus in
great anger slew him, and in menacing wise added these words
withal, "So perish whoever else shall leap over my walls!" Thus
Romulus acquired sole power, and the city, thus founded, was
called by its founder's name.

Livy, *Ab urbe condita* 1.6–7

II. Conditā cīvitāte, quam ex nōmine suō Rōmam vocāvit, haec ferē ēgit:
multitūdinem fīnitimōrum in cīvitātem recēpit, centum ex seniōribus
lēgit, quōrum cōnsiliō omnia ageret, quōs senātōrēs nōmināvit propter
senectūtem. Tum, cum uxōrēs ipse et populus suus nōn habērent, invītāvit
ad spectāculum lūdōrum vīcīnās urbī Rōmae nātiōnēs atque eārum vir-

10

---

7. **Conditā cīvitāte** – *with the city having been founded = after the city had been
founded.*
ferē – *approximately, more or less.*

8. **centum ex seniōribus** – *one hundred from the elders = one hundred of the
elders.*

9. **quōrum cōnsiliō** – *by whose advice.*

11. **vīcīnās urbī Rōmae** – *neighboring [to] the city Rome.*

ginēs rapuit. Commōtīs bellīs propter raptārum iniūriam Caenīnēnsēs vīcit, Antemnātēs, Crustumīnōs, Sabīnōs, Fīdēnātēs, Vēientēs. Haec omnia oppida urbem cingunt.

THE RAPE OF THE SABINE WOMEN

When the time came for the show, and people's thoughts and eyes were busy with it, the preconcerted attack began. At a given signal the young Romans darted this way and that, to seize and carry off the maidens. In most cases these were taken by the men in whose path they chanced to be. Some, of exceptional beauty, had been marked out for the chief senators, and were carried off to their houses by plebeians to whom the office had been entrusted. . . . The sports broke up in a panic, and the parents of the maidens fled sorrowing. They charged the Romans with the crime of violating hospitality, and invoked the gods to whose solemn games they had come, deceived in violation of religion and honour. The stolen maidens were no more hopeful of their plight, nor less indignant. But Romulus himself went amongst them and explained that the pride of their parents had caused this deed, when they had refused their neighbours the right to intermarry; nevertheless the daughters should be wedded and become co-partners in all the possessions of the Romans, in their citizenship and, dearest privilege of all to the human race, in their children; only let them moderate their anger, and give their hearts to those to whom fortune had given their persons. A sense of injury had often given place to affection, and they would find their husbands the kinder for this reason, that every man would earnestly endeavour not only to be a good husband, but also to console his wife for the home and parents she had lost.

Livy, *Ab urbe condita* 1.9

---

12. **Commōtīs bellīs** – *with war having been stirred up* = *when war broke out.*
propter raptārum iniūriam – *on account of the outrage of the [maidens] having been carried off.*

15   Et cum, ortā subitō tempestāte, nōn compāruisset, annō rēgnī trīcēsimō
     septimō ad deōs trānsīsse crēditus est et cōnsecrātus. Deinde Rōmae per
     quīnōs diēs senātōrēs imperāvērunt et hīs rēgnantibus annus ūnus com-
     plētus est.

THE DEATH OF ROMULUS

When these deathless deeds had been done, as the king was holding a muster in the Campus Martius, near the swamp of Capra, for
the purpose of reviewing the army, suddenly a storm came up, with
loud claps of thunder, and enveloped him in a cloud so thick as to
hide him from the sight of the assembly; and from that moment
Romulus was no more on earth. The Roman soldiers at length recovered from their panic, when this hour of wild confusion had
been succeeded by a sunny calm; but when they saw that the royal
seat was empty, although they readily believed the assertion of the
senators, who had been standing next to Romulus, that he had
been caught up on high in the blast, they nevertheless remained for
some time sorrowful and silent, as if filled with the fear of orphan-
hood. Then, when a few men had taken the initiative, they all with
one accord hailed Romulus as a god and a god's son, the King and
Father of the Roman City.

Livy, *Ab urbe condita* 1.16

---

15. **nōn compāruisset** – *he had not appeared.*
     annō . . . trīcēsimō septimō – *in the thirty-seventh year.*
16. **trānsīsse crēditus est** – *he was thought to have crossed over.*
     cōnsecrātus = *cōnsecrātus est.*
     Rōmae – *at Rome* (also at line 23).
     per quīnōs diēs – *for five days each.*
17. **hīs rēgnantibus** – *with these reigning* = *under their rule.*

Numa Pompilius, 715–672 BCE

III. Posteā Numa Pompilius rēx creātus est, quī bellum quidem nūllum gessit, sed nōn minus cīvitātī quam Rōmulus prōfuit. Nam et lēgēs 20 Rōmānīs mōrēsque cōnstituit, quī cōnsuētūdine proeliōrum iam latrōnēs ac sēmibarbarī putābantur, et annum dēscrīpsit in decem mēnsēs prius sine aliquā supputātiōne cōnfūsum, et īnfīnīta Rōmae sacra ac templa cōnstituit. Morbō dēcessit quadrāgēsimō et tertiō imperiī annō.

NUMA'S ACHIEVEMENTS

When he had thus obtained the kingship, he prepared to give the new City, founded by force of arms, a new foundation in law, statutes, and observances. . . . He thought the very first thing to do, as being the most efficacious with a populace which was ignorant and, in those early days, uncivilized, was to imbue them with the fear of Heaven. . . . But of all his services the greatest was this, that throughout his reign he guarded peace no less jealously than his kingdom. Thus two successive kings in different ways, one by war, the other by peace, promoted the nation's welfare. Romulus ruled

---

continued

19. **quidem** – *indeed.*
20. **nōn minus cīvitātī . . . prōfuit** – *was no less beneficial to the city.*
21. **cōnsuētūdine proeliōrum** – *because of their habit of [waging] wars.*
    iam . . . putābantur – *were now beginning to be thought.*
22. **annum dēscrīpsit in decem mēnsēs** – *fixed the year into ten months.*
    prius sine aliquā supputātiōne cōnfūsum – *[which had been] previously confused without any [method of] computation.*
23. **aliquā supputātiōne** = *ūllā supputātiōne.*
    īnfīnīta . . . sacra – *innumerable sacred rites.*
24. **Morbō** – *by a disease* = *by natural causes.*
    dēcessit – *died.*
    quadrāgēsimō et tertiō . . . annō – *in the forty-third year.*

> thirty-seven years, Numa forty-three. The state was not only strong,
> but was also well organized in the arts both of war and of peace.
>
> Livy, *Ab urbe condita* 1.19–21

Tullus Hostilius, 672–642 BCE

25 IV. Huic successit Tullus Hostīlius. Hic bella reparāvit, Albānōs vīcit, quī ab urbe Rōmā duodecimō mīliāriō sunt, Vēientēs et Fīdēnātēs, quōrum aliī sextō mīliāriō absunt ab urbe Rōmā, aliī octāvō decimō, bellō superāvit, urbem ampliāvit, adiectō Caeliō monte. Cum trīgintā et duōs annōs rēgnāsset, fulmine ictus cum domō suā ārsit.

> THE CHARACTER OF TULLUS HOSTILIUS
>
> This monarch was not only unlike the last, but was actually more warlike than Romulus had been. Besides his youth and strength, the glory of his grandfather [Hostus Hostilius] was also an incentive to him. So, thinking that the nation was growing decrepit from inaction, he everywhere sought excuses for stirring up war.
>
> Livy, *Ab urbe condita* 1.22

25. **Huic successit** – *succeeded him.*
    reparāvit – *renewed.*
26. **ab urbe Rōmā duodecimō mīliāriō** – *at the twelfth mile marker from the city Rome = twelve miles from Rome.*
    quōrum – *of whom.*
27. **aliī . . . aliī** – *the one . . . the other.*
    octāvō decimō = *octāvō decimō mīliāriō, at the eighteenth mile marker.*
    bellō – *in war.*
28. **adiectō** – *having been added.*
29. **rēgnāsset** = *rēgnāvisset.*
    fulmine ictus – *having been struck by lightning = after he had been struck by lightning.*
    cum domō suā – *together with his house.*

Ancus Marcius, 642–616 BCE

V. Post hunc Ancus Mārcius, Numae ex fīliā nepōs, suscēpit imperium.   30
Contrā Latīnōs dīmicāvit, Aventīnum montem cīvitātī adiēcit et Iāniculum, apud ōstium Tiberis cīvitātem suprā mare sextō decimō mīliāriō ab
urbe Rōmā condidit. Vīcēsimō et quārtō annō imperiī morbō periit.

AN ETRUSCAN ENTERS ROME

In the reign of Ancus one Lucumo, a man of energy and wealth,
took up his residence in Rome, chiefly from ambition and the hope
that he might there achieve a station such as he had found no opportunity of attaining in Tarquinii. . . . [He and his wife Tanaquil]
had come, as it happened, as far as Janiculum, when, as they were
sitting in their covered waggon, an eagle poised on its wings gently
descended upon them and plucked off Lucumo's cap, after which,
rising noisily above the car and again stooping, as if sent from
heaven for that service, it deftly replaced the cap upon his head,
and departed on high. This augury was joyfully accepted, it is said,
by Tanaquil, who was a woman skilled in celestial prodigies, as was
the case with most Etruscans. Embracing her husband, she bade
him expect transcendent greatness: such was the meaning of that
bird, appearing from that quarter of the sky, and bringing tidings
from that god; the highest part of the man had been concerned in
the omen; the eagle had removed the adornment placed upon a
mortal's head that it might restore it with the divine approbation.
Such were their hopes and their reflections as they entered the City.

---

continued

30. **Numae ex fīliā nepōs** = *nepōs Numae ex fīliā.*
31. **dīmicāvit** – *fought.*
32. **ōstium Tiberis** – *mouth of the Tiber.*
    suprā mare – *above the sea = on the seacoast.*
    sextō decimō – *sixteenth.*
33. **Vīcēsimō et quārtō** – *twenty-fourth.*

> Having obtained a house, they gave out the name of Lucius Tar-
> quinius Priscus. The Romans regarded him with special interest, as
> a stranger and a man of wealth, and he steadily pushed his fortune
> by his own exertions, making friends wherever possible, by kind
> words, courteous hospitality, and benefactions, until his reputation
> extended even to the palace.
>
> Livy, *Ab urbe condita* 1.34

Tarquinius Priscus, 616–579 BCE

VI. Deinde rēgnum Prīscus Tarquinius accēpit. Hic numerum senātōrum
35   duplicāvit, circum Rōmae aedificāvit, lūdōs Rōmānōs īnstituit, quī ad
nostram memoriam permanent. Vīcit īdem etiam Sabīnōs et nōn parum
agrōrum sublātum īsdem urbis Rōmae territōriō iūnxit, prīmusque triumphāns urbem intrāvit. Mūrōs fēcit et cloācās, Capitōlium inchoāvit.
Trīcēsimō octāvō imperiī annō per Ancī fīliōs occīsus est, rēgis eius cuī
40   ipse successerat.

35. **ad nostram memoriam** = *ad nostram aetatem.*
36. **permanent** – *continue.*
    īdem – *furthermore.*
    nōn parum – *not a small amount* = *a large amount.*
37. **sublātum** – *[having been] taken.*
    īsdem = *eīsdem, from the same,* i.e., from the Sabines.
    urbis Rōmae territōriō – *to the territory of the city [of] Rome.*
    prīmusque – *and [he was] the first.*
    triumphāns – *in a triumphal procession.*
38. **Mūrōs** = *mūrōs urbis.*
    cloācās – *underground drains.*
    inchoāvit – *began [construction of].*
39. **Trīcēsimō octāvō** – *thirty-eighth.*
    Ancī . . . , rēgis eius cuī ipse successerat – *of Ancus, that king whom he himself had succeeded.*

PRODIGIUM VISU EVENTUQUE MIRABILE

At this time there happened in the house of the king a portent which
was remarkable alike in its manifestation and in its outcome. The story
is that while a child named Servius Tullius lay sleeping, his head burst
into flames in the sight of many. The general outcry which so great a
miracle called forth brought the king [Tarquinius] and queen [Tana-
quil] to the place. One of the servants fetched water to quench the fire,
but was checked by the queen, who stilled the uproar and commanded
that the boy should not be disturbed until he awoke of himself. Soon
afterwards sleep left him, and with it disappeared the flames. Then,
taking her husband aside, Tanaquil said: "Do you see this child whom
we are bringing up in so humble a fashion? Be assured he will one day
be a lamp to our dubious fortunes, and a protector to the royal house
in the day of its distress. Let us therefore rear with all solicitude one
who will lend high renown to the state and to our family."

Livy, *Ab urbe condita* 1.39

Servius Tullius, 579–534 BCE

VII. Post hunc Servius Tullius suscēpit imperium, genitus ex nōbilī
fēminā, captīvā tamen et ancillā. Hic quoque Sabīnōs subēgit, montēs
trēs, Quirīnālem, Vīminālem, Ēsquilīnum, urbī adiūnxit, fossās circum
mūrum dūxit. Prīmus omnium cēnsum ōrdināvit, quī adhūc per orbem
terrārum incognitus erat. Sub eō, Rōma, omnibus in cēnsum dēlātīs,   45

41. **genitus** – *born.*
42. **subēgit** – *subdued.*
44. **dūxit** – *constructed.*
    Prīmus . . . ōrdināvit – *he was the first to carry out.*
    orbem terrārum – *the circle of lands = the earth.*
45. **Sub eō** – *under him.*
    omnibus . . . dēlātīs – *with all having been registered = when everyone had
    been registered.*

habuit capita LXXXIII mīlia cīvium Rōmānōrum cum hīs quī in agrīs erant. Occīsus est scelere generī suī Tarquiniī Superbī, fīliī eius rēgis, cuī ipse successerat, et fīliae, quam Tarquinius habēbat uxōrem.

Tarquinius Superbus, 534–510 BCE

VIII. L. Tarquinius Superbus, septimus atque ultimus rēgum, Volscōs,
50 quae gēns ad Campāniam euntibus nōn longē ab urbe est, vīcit, Gabiōs cīvitātem et Suessam Pōmētiam subēgit, cum Tuscīs pācem fēcit et templum Iovis in Capitōliō aedificāvit. Posteā, Ardeam oppugnāns, in octāvō decimō mīliāriō ab urbe Rōmā positam cīvitātem, imperium perdidit. Nam cum fīlius eius, et ipse Tarquinius iūnior, nōbilissimam fēminam
55 Lucrētiam eandemque pudīcissimam, Collātīnī uxōrem, stuprāsset eaque

46. **capita LXXXIII mīlia cīvium Rōmānōrum** – *eighty-three thousand (heads of) Roman citizens.*
     cum hīs quī in agrīs erant – *[together] with those who were in the country.*
47. **scelere generī suī . . . et fīliae** – *by the crime of his son-in-law and daughter.*
48. **habēbat uxōrem** – *had as a wife.*
49. **L.** = *Lucius.*
     rēgum – *of the kings.*
50. **quae gēns . . . est** – *which is a people.*
     ad Campāniam euntibus – *for those going to Campania = as one heads south from Rome.*
     Gabiōs cīvitātem et Suessam Pōmētiam – *the city Gabii and [the city] Suessa Pometia.*
51. **subēgit** – *subdued.*
     Tuscīs = *Etruscīs.*
52. **octāvō decimō** – *eighteenth.*
53. **positam** – *situated.*
     perdidit – *lost.*
54. **et ipse Tarquinius iūnior** – *and he himself [was called] Tarquinius the Younger.*
55. **eandemque** – *and also.*
     stuprāsset = *stuprāvisset, had violated.*
     eaque . . . questa fuisset – *and [when] she had complained.*

dē iniūriā marītō et patrī et amīcīs questa fuisset, in omnium cōnspectū
sē occīdit. Propter quam causam Brūtus, parēns et ipse Tarquiniī, populum concitāvit et Tarquiniō adēmit imperium. Mox exercitus quoque eum,
quī cīvitātem Ardeam cum ipsō rēge oppugnābat, relīquit; veniēnsque ad
urbem rēx, portīs clausīs, exclūsus est, cumque imperāsset annōs quat-   60
tuor et vīgintī cum uxōre et līberīs suīs fūgit. Ita Rōmae rēgnātum est per
septem rēgēs annīs ducentīs quadrāgintā tribus, cum adhūc Rōma, ubi
plūrimum, vix ūsque ad quīntum decimum mīliārium possidēret.

GRIEF WAS SWALLOWED UP IN ANGER

Brutus, while the others were absorbed in grief, drew out the knife
from Lucretia's wound, and holding it up, dripping with gore, ex-
claimed, "By this blood, most chaste until a prince wronged it, I

---

continued

56. **in . . . cōnspectū** – *in the sight.*
57. **Propter quam causam** = *et propter hanc causam.*
    parēns et ipse Tarquiniī – *he himself also a relative of Tarquinius.*
58. **concitāvit** – *incited.*
    Tarquiniō adēmit – *took from Tarquinius.*
59. **relīquit** – *deserted.*
60. **exclūsus est** – *he was shut out.*
    cumque – *and when.*
    imperāsset = *imperāvisset, had reigned.*
    quattuor et vīgintī – *twenty-four.*
61. **līberīs suīs** – *his children.*
    Rōmae rēgnātum est – *it was ruled at Rome* = *Rome was ruled.*
    per – *by.*
62. **annīs ducentīs quadrāgintā tribus** = *annōs ducentōs quadrāgintā trēs, for*
    243 years.
    cum adhūc Rōma . . . vix . . . possidēret – *while as yet Rome barely occupied*
    [land].
    ubi plūrimum – *where most* = *at the most.*
63. **ūsque ad** – *as far as.*

swear, and I take you, gods, to witness, that I will pursue Lucius
Tarquinius Superbus and his wicked wife and all his children, with
sword, with fire, aye with whatsoever violence I may; and that I will
suffer neither them nor any other to be king in Rome!" The knife he
then passed to Collatinus, and from him to Lucretius and Valerius.
They were dumbfounded at this miracle. Whence came this new
spirit in the breast of Brutus [who had been feigning madness]? As
he bade them, so they swore. Grief was swallowed up in anger; and
when Brutus summoned them to make war from that very moment
on the power of the kings, they followed his lead.

Livy, *Ab urbe condita* 1.59

Founding of the Republic, 509 BCE

IX. Hinc cōnsulēs coepēre, prō ūnō rēge duo, hāc causā creātī, ut, sī ūnus

65 malus esse voluisset, alter eum, habēns potestātem similem, coercēret. Et
placuit, nē imperium longius quam annuum habērent, nē per diūturnitātem potestātis īnsolentiōrēs redderentur, sed cīvīlēs semper essent, quī

64. **Hinc** – *from this point forward.*
   cōnsulēs coepēre . . . creātī – *consuls began to be elected.*
   coepēre = *coepērunt.*
   prō ūnō rēge duo – *in place of one king, two [consuls].*
   hāc causā – *for the following reason.*
   sī ūnus malus esse voluisset – *if one were disposed to be unjust.*
65. **alter eum . . . coercēret** – *the other would restrain him.*
66. **placuit** – *it was resolved.*
   nē . . . habērent . . . sed . . . essent – *that they should not hold . . . but should be.*
   annuum – *for one year.*
   nē . . . redderentur – *lest they become.*
   diūturnitātem potestātis – *long duration of power.*
67. **īnsolentiōrēs** – *too arrogant.*
   cīvīlēs – *like [regular] citizens.*
   quī sē . . . scīrent futūrōs esse – *who would know that they would be.*

Jacques-Louis David, *The Intervention of the Sabine Women*, 1799. Oil on canvas.
Louvre Museum, via Wikimedia Commons.

sē post annum scīrent futūrōs esse prīvātōs. Fuērunt igitur, annō prīmō
expulsīs rēgibus, cōnsulēs L. Iūnius Brūtus, quī maximē ēgerat ut Tarquinius pellerētur, et Tarquinius Collātīnus, marītus Lucrētiae. Sed Tarquiniō 70
Collātīnō statim sublāta est dignitās. Placuerat enim, nē quisquam in urbe
remanēret quī Tarquinius vocārētur. Ergō, acceptō omnī patrimōniō suō,
ex urbe migrāvit, et locō ipsīus factus est L. Valerius Pūblicola cōnsul.

68. **prīvātōs** – *private individuals.*
69. **L.** = *Lucius.*
   maximē ēgerat – *had done the most.*
70. **Tarquiniō Collātīnō** – *from Tarquinius Collatinus.*
71. **dignitās** – *dignity [of public office].*
   Placuerat – *it had been resolved.*
72. **acceptō omnī patrimōniō suō** – *with his personal property having been collected.*
73. **locō ipsīus** – *in his place.*

Commōvit tamen bellum urbī Rōmae rēx Tarquinius, quī fuerat expulsus,
75   et collēctīs multīs gentibus, ut in rēgnum posset restituī dīmicāvit.

To Regain His Country and His Sovereignty

[Tarquinius Superbus] believed it was time to contrive an open war.
He therefore went about as a suppliant amongst the cities of Etruria,
directing his prayers chiefly to the Veientes and the Tarquinienses.
Reminding them that he had come from them and was of the same
blood as themselves, and that exile and poverty had followed hard
upon his loss of what had been but now great power, he besought
them not to let him perish, with his youthful sons, before their very
eyes. . . . He himself, while actually king, and enlarging Rome's sway
by war, had been driven out by his next-of-kin in a wicked conspiracy.
His enemies, perceiving that no single claimant was fit to be king,
had seized and usurped the power amongst themselves, and had
given up his goods to be plundered by the people, that none might
be without a share in the guilt. He wished to regain his country and
his sovereignty, and to punish the ungrateful Romans. . . . So it came
about that two armies, representing two nations, followed Tarquinius, to regain his kingdom for him and to chastise the Romans.

Livy, *Ab urbe condita* 2.6

War with Tarquinius Superbus, 509 BCE

X. In prīmā pugnā Brūtus cōnsul et Arrūns, Tarquiniī fīlius, in vicem
sē occīdērunt, Rōmānī tamen ex eā pugnā victōrēs recessērunt. Brūtum

74. **urbī Rōmae** – *against the city [of] Rome.*
    fuerat expulsus = *expulsus erat.*
75. **restituī** – *to be restored.*
    dīmicāvit – *fought.*
76. **in vicem sē** – *each other in turn.*
77. **victōrēs** – *victorious.*
    recessērunt – *withdrew.*

mātrōnae Rōmānae, dēfēnsōrem pudīcitiae suae, quasi commūnem patrem per annum lūxērunt. Valerius Pūblicola Sp. Lucrētium Tricipitīnum collēgam sibi fēcit, Lucrētiae patrem, quō morbō mortuō iterum Horā- 80 tium Pulvillum collēgam sibi sūmpsit. Ita prīmus annus quīnque cōnsulēs habuit, cum Tarquinius Collātīnus propter nōmen urbe cessisset, Brūtus in proeliō perīsset, Sp. Lucrētius morbō mortuus esset.

War with Lars Porsenna, 508 BCE

XI. Secundō quoque annō iterum Tarquinius, ut reciperētur in rēgnum, bellum Rōmānīs intulit, auxilium eī ferente Porsennā, Tusciae rēge, et 85 Rōmam paene cēpit. Vērum tum quoque victus est. Tertiō annō post rēgēs exāctōs, Tarquinius, cum suscipī nōn posset in rēgnum neque eī Porsenna, quī pācem cum Rōmānīs fēcerat, praestāret auxilium, Tusculum sē

78. **dēfēnsōrem** – *defender.*
    pudīcitiae suae – *their honor.*
79. **lūxērunt** – *mourned.*
    Sp. = *Spurium.*
80. **collēgam sibi** – *his colleague.*
    quō morbō mortuō = *et eō morbō mortuō.*
    morbō – *by a disease* = *by natural causes.*
    iterum – *in turn.*
81. **sūmpsit** – *selected.*
82. **cessisset** – *had left.*
83. **perīsset** = *periisset.*
84. **ut reciperētur in rēgnum** – *to be returned to power.*
85. **Tusciae** = *Etruriae.*
86. **Vērum** – *but.*
    post rēgēs exāctōs – *after the kings [had been] expelled.*
87. **cum suscipī nōn posset** – *since he could not be readmitted.*
    neque eī Porsenna . . . praestāret auxilium – *nor was Porsenna offering him help.*
88. **sē contulit** – *he betook himself* = *he took refuge.*

contulit, quae cīvitās nōn longē ab urbe est, atque ibi per quattuordecim
90   annōs prīvātus cum uxōre cōnsenuit.

ROMANUS SUM CIVIS

Gaius Mucius, a young Roman noble, thinking it a shame that although the Roman People had not, in the days of their servitude
when they lived under kings, been blockaded in a war by any enemies, they should now, when free, be besieged by those same Etruscans whose armies they had so often routed, made up his mind that
this indignity must be avenged by some great and daring deed. At
first he intended to make his way to the enemy's camp on his own
account. . . . Hiding a sword under his dress, he set out. Arrived
at the camp, he took up his stand in the thick of the crowd near
the royal tribunal. It happened that at that moment the soldiers were
being paid; a secretary who sat beside the king, and wore nearly the
same costume, was very busy, and to him the soldiers for the most part
addressed themselves. Mucius was afraid to ask which was Porsinna,
lest his ignorance of the king's identity should betray his own, and following the blind guidance of Fortune, slew the secretary instead of the
king. . . . There was an outcry, and thereat the royal guards came running in from every side, seized him and dragged him back before the
tribunal of the king. But friendless as he was, even then, when Fortune
wore so menacing an aspect, yet as one more to be feared than fearing,
"I am a Roman citizen," he cried; "men call me Gaius Mucius. I am
your enemy, and as an enemy I would have slain you; I can die as res-
olutely as I could kill: both to do and to endure valiantly is the Roman
way. Nor am I the only one to carry this resolution against you: behind
me is a long line of men who are seeking the same honour. . . . Such is

---

89. **quae cīvitās** – *a city which*.
   quattuordecim – *fourteen*.
90. **prīvātus** – *a private citizen*.
   cōnsenuit – *grew old*.

> the war we, the Roman youths, declare on you. . . ." The king, at once
> hot with resentment and aghast at his danger, angrily ordered the pris-
> oner to be flung into the flames unless he should at once divulge the
> plot with which he so obscurely threatened him. Whereupon Mucius,
> exclaiming, "Look, that you may see how cheap they hold their bodies
> whose eyes are fixed upon renown!" thrust his hand into the fire that
> was kindled for the sacrifice.
>
> Livy, *Ab urbe condita* 2.12

Quārtō annō post rēgēs exāctōs, cum Sabīnī Rōmānīs bellum intulissent,
victī sunt et dē hīs triumphātum est. Quīntō annō L. Valerius ille, Brūtī
collēga et quater cōnsul, fātāliter mortuus est, adeō pauper ut, collātīs ā
populō nummīs, sūmptum habuerit sepultūrae. Quem mātrōnae sīcutī
Brūtum annum lūxērunt.   95

The Dictatorship, 501 BCE

XII. Nōnō annō post rēgēs exāctōs, cum gener Tarquiniī ad iniūriam socerī vindicandam ingentem collēgisset exercitum, nova Rōmae dignitās

92. **dē hīs triumphātum est** – *a triumph was celebrated over them.*
    L. Valerius ille – *the famous Lucius Valerius.*
93. **quater** – *four times.*
    fātāliter – *according to fate = naturally.*
    collātīs ā populō nummīs – *with money having been collected from the people.*
94. **sūmptum habuerit sepultūrae** – *bore the expenses of his funeral.*
    Quem = *et eum.*
95. **lūxērunt** – *mourned.*
96. **gener** – *son-in-law.*
    ad iniūriam socerī vindicandam – *to avenge the wrong done to his father-in-law.*
97. **collēgisset** – *had collected.*
    Rōmae – *at Rome* (also at lines 100 and 101).
    dignitās – *political office.*

est creāta, quae dictātūra appellātur, maior quam cōnsulātus. Eōdem annō
etiam magister equitum factus est, quī dictātōrī obsequerētur. Dictātor
100 autem Rōmae prīmus fuit T. Larcius, magister equitum prīmus Sp. Cassius.

Secession of the Plebeians, 494 BCE

XIII. Sextō decimō annō post rēgēs exāctōs, sēditiōnem populus Rōmae
fēcit, tamquam ā senātū atque cōnsulibus premerētur. Tum et ipse sibi
tribūnōs plēbis quasi propriōs iūdicēs et dēfēnsōrēs creāvit, per quōs contrā senātum et cōnsulēs tūtus esse posset.

THE FABLE OF AGRIPPA MENENIUS

[The senate] therefore decided to send as an ambassador to the
commons Agrippa Menenius, an eloquent man and dear to the plebeians as being one of themselves by birth. On being admitted to
the camp he is said merely to have related the following apologue,
in the quaint and uncouth style of that age: In the days when man's
members did not all agree amongst themselves, as is now the case,
but had each its own ideas and a voice of its own, the other parts
thought it unfair that they should have the worry and the trouble

---

98. **est creāta** = *creāta est.*
    dictātūra – *dictatorship.*
    maior – *more powerful.*
    cōnsulātus – *consulship.*
99. **magister equitum** – *master of the horse.*
    quī dictātōrī obsequerētur – *to be subordinate to the dictator.*
100. **T.** = *Titus.*
    magister equitum prīmus = *magister equitum prīmus fuit.*
    Sp. = *Spurius.*
101. **sēditiōnem . . . fēcit** – *made a rebellion.*
102. **tamquam . . . premerētur** – *on the grounds that they were oppressed.*
    ipse – *[the people] itself* = *they themselves.*
103. **quasi propriōs iūdicēs** – *as their own judges.*

and the labour of providing everything for the belly, while the belly remained quietly in their midst with nothing to do but to enjoy the good things which they bestowed upon it; they therefore conspired together that the hands should carry no food to the mouth, nor the mouth accept anything that was given it, nor the teeth grind up what they received. While they sought in this angry spirit to starve the belly into submission, the members themselves and the whole body were reduced to the utmost weakness. Hence it had become clear that even the belly had no idle task to perform, and was no more nourished than it nourished the rest, by giving out to all parts of the body that by which we live and thrive, when it has been divided equally amongst the veins and is enriched with digested food—that is, the blood. Drawing a parallel from this to show how like was the internal dissension of the bodily members to the anger of the plebs against the Fathers, he prevailed upon the minds of his hearers.

Livy, *Ab urbe condita* 2.32

War with the Volsci, 493 BCE

XIV. Sequentī annō Volscī contrā Rōmānōs bellum reparāvērunt, et victī   105
aciē etiam Coriolōs cīvitātem, quam habēbant optimam, perdidērunt.

Coriolanus, 491 BCE

XV. Octāvō decimō annō postquam rēgēs ēiectī erant, expulsus ex urbe
Q. Mārcius, dux Rōmānus, quī Coriolōs cēperat, Volscōrum cīvitātem, ad
ipsōs Volscōs contendit īrātus et auxilia contrā Rōmānōs accēpit. Rōmānōs

105. **reparāvērunt** – *renewed.*
    victī aciē – *having been conquered in battle.*
106. **quam habēbant optimam** = *optimam quam habēbant.*
107. **expulsus** – *having been expelled from the city.*
108. **Q.** = *Quīntus.*
109. **contendit īrātus** – *in anger went over.*

110 saepe vīcit, ūsque ad quīntum mīliārium urbis accessit, oppugnātūrus
etiam patriam suam, lēgātīs quī pācem petēbant repudiātīs, nisi ad eum
māter Veturia et uxor Volumnia ex urbe vēnissent, quārum flētū et dēprecātiōne superātus remōvit exercitum. Atque hic secundus post Tarquinium fuit, quī dux contrā patriam suam esset.

Disaster at Cremera, 479 BCE

115 XVI. C. Fabiō et L. Virgīniō cōnsulibus, trecentī nōbilēs hominēs, quī ex
Fabiā familiā erant, contrā Vēientēs bellum sōlī suscēpērunt, prōmittentēs
senātuī et populō per sē omne certāmen implendum. Itaque profectī,
omnēs nōbilēs et quī singulī magnōrum exercituum ducēs esse dēbērent,
in proeliō concidērunt. Ūnus omnīnō superfuit ex tantā familiā, quī prop-
120 ter aetātem puerīlem dūcī nōn potuerat ad pugnam. Post haec cēnsus in
urbe habitus est et inventa sunt cīvium capita CXVII mīlia CCCXIX.

---

110. **accessit** – *reached.*
    oppugnātūrus – *ready to attack* = *oppugnāvisset, would have attacked.*
111. **lēgātīs . . . repudiātīs** – *the ambassadors having been rejected.*
112. **quārum flētū et dēprecātiōne superātus** – *overcome by their weeping and*
    entreaty.
115. **C.** = *Gaiō.*
    L. = *Luciō.*
117. **per sē** – *on their own.*
    omne certāmen implendum = *omne certāmen implendum esse, the entire*
    battle would be carried out.
    profectī – *having marched out.*
118. **quī singulī . . . ducēs esse dēbērent** – *every single one of whom should have*
    been a commander.
119. **concidērunt** – *fell.*
    omnīnō – *in all.*
    superfuit – *survived.*
120. **puerīlem** – *youthful.*
    dūcī – *to be taken.*
    Post haec – *after these things = after this.*
121. **cīvium capita CXVII mīlia CCCXIX** – *117,319 (heads of) Roman citizens.*

The Last Stand of the Three Hundred Fabii

As the Etruscans drew together and the Romans were now fenced in by a continuous line of armed men, the harder the enemy pressed them the smaller was the space within which they themselves were forced to contract their circle, a thing which clearly revealed both their own fewness and the vast numbers of the Etruscans, whose ranks were multiplied in the narrow space. The Romans then gave up the fight which they had been directing equally at every point, and all turned in one direction. Thither, by dint of main strength and arms, they forced their way with a wedge. Their road led up a gentle acclivity. There they at first made a stand; presently, when their superior position had afforded them time to breathe and to collect their spirits after so great a fright, they actually routed the troops which were advancing to dislodge them; and a handful of men, with the aid of a good position, were winning the victory, when the Veientes who had been sent round by the ridge emerged upon the crest of the hill, thus giving the enemy the advantage again. The Fabii were all slain to a man, and their fort was stormed. Three hundred and six men perished, as is generally agreed; one, who was little more than a boy in years, survived to maintain the Fabian stock, and so to afford the very greatest help to the Roman People in its dark hours, on many occasions, at home and in the field.

Livy, *Ab urbe condita* 2.50

Cincinnatus, 458 BCE

XVII. Sequentī annō cum in Algidō monte ab urbe duodecimō fermē mīliāriō Rōmānus obsidērētur exercitus, L. Quīntius Cincinnātus dictātor

122. **Algidō monte** – *Mount Algidus.*
     duodecimō – *twelve.*
     fermē – *about.*
123. **obsidērētur** – *was blockaded.*
     L. = *Lucius.*

est factus, quī agrum quattuor iūgerum possidēns manibus suīs colēbat.
125   Is cum in opere et arāns esset inventus, sūdōre dētersō togam praetextam
accēpit et caesīs hostibus līberāvit exercitum.

The Decemviri, 451–449 BCE

XVIII. Annō trecentēsimō et alterō ab urbe conditā imperium cōnsulāre cessāvit et prō duōbus cōnsulibus decem factī sunt, quī summam
potestātem habērent, decemvirī nōminātī. Sed cum prīmō annō bene
130   ēgissent, secundō ūnus ex hīs, Ap. Claudius, Virgīniī cuiusdam, quī honestīs iam stīpendiīs contrā Latīnōs in monte Algidō mīlitārat, filiam virginem corrumpere voluit; quam pater occīdit, nē stuprum ā decemvirō

124. **est factus** = *factus est.*
     quattuor iūgerūm – *of four iugera,* i.e., 2.8 acres.
125. **in opere et arāns** – *at work and plowing* = *at work with his plow.*
     esset inventus = *inventus esset.*
     sūdōre dētersō – *with his sweat being wiped away.*
127. **trecentēsimō et alterō** = *trecentēsimō et secundō, 302nd.*
     ab urbe conditā – *from the city having been founded* = *from the foundation of the city.*
     imperium cōnsulāre – *consular power.*
128. **decem** = *decem virī.*
     factī sunt – *were appointed.*
     quī . . . habērent – *to hold.*
129. **nōminātī** – *called.*
     cum – *although.*
130. **secundō** = *secundō annō.*
     Ap. = *Appius.*
     Virgīniī cuiusdam . . . filiam virginem – *the unmarried daughter of a certain Virginius.*
     honestīs . . . stīpendiīs – *in honorable service.*
131. **mīlitārat** = *mīlitāverat.*
132. **corrumpere** – *to defile.*
     quam = *et eam.*
     stuprum . . . sustinēret – *endure dishonor.*

sustinēret, et regressus ad mīlitēs mōvit tumultum. Sublāta est decemvirīs potestās ipsīque damnātī sunt.

They Were Men, and Armed

As Verginius spoke these words in a loud voice, the multitude sig-
nified with responsive shouts that they would not forget his suffer-
ings nor fail to vindicate their liberty. And the civilians, mingling
with the crowd, repeated the same complaints and told them how
much more shameful the thing would have appeared if they could
have seen it instead of hearing about it. . . . They induced the troops
to raise the cry "To arms!" and to pluck up their standards and set
out for Rome. The decemvirs, troubled alike by what they saw and
by what they heard had taken place in Rome, rushed through the
camp, one this way, another that, to still the rising. And so long as
they mildly remonstrated, they got no answer; but if one of them tried
to use his authority, they told him that they were men, and armed.

Livy, *Ab urbe condita* 3.50

Revolt of Fidenae, 438 BCE

XIX. Annō trecentēsimō et quīntō decimō ab urbe conditā Fīdēnātēs con-   135
trā Rōmānōs rebellāvērunt. Auxilium hīs praestābant Vēientēs et rēx Vēien-
tium Tolumnius. Quae ambae cīvitātēs tam vīcīnae urbī sunt ut Fīdēnae
sextō, Vēī octāvō decimō mīliāriō absint. Coniūnxērunt sē hīs et Volscī.

---

133. **regressus** – *having returned* = *after he returned.*
     mōvit tumultum – *stirred up a rebellion.*
     decemvirīs – *from the Decemviri.*
134. **damnātī sunt** – *were condemned.*
135. **trecentēsimō et quīntō decimō** – *315th.*
137. **Quae ambae** = *et eae ambae, and both these.*
     tam vīcīnae urbī – *so near to the city.*
138. **Coniūnxērunt sē . . . Volscī** – *the Volsci joined themselves.*
     et = *etiam.*

Sed Mam. Aemiliō dictātōre et L. Quīntiō Cincinnātō magistrō equitum,
140   victī etiam rēgem perdidērunt. Fīdēnae captae et excīsae.

War with Veii, 396 BCE

XX. Post vīgintī deinde annōs Vēientānī rebellāvērunt. Dictātor contrā
ipsōs missus est Fūrius Camillus, quī prīmum eōs vīcit aciē, mox etiam
cīvitātem diū obsidēns cēpit, antīquissimam Ītaliaeque dītissimam. Post
eam, cēpit et Faliscōs, nōn minus nōbilem cīvitātem. Sed commōta est eī
145   invidia, quasi praedam male dīvīsisset, damnātusque ob eam causam et
expulsus cīvitāte.

THE ROMANS TUNNEL INTO VEII'S CITADEL AND INTERRUPT A
SACRIFICE TO JUNO

At this point men introduce a tale, how, as the King of the Veientes
was sacrificing, the Roman soldiers in the mine overheard the
soothsayer declare that to him who should cut up the inwards of

---

139. **Mam.** = *Māmercō.*
     L. = *Luciō.*
140. **victī** – *having been conquered.*
     perdidērunt – *they lost.*
     captae et excīsae = *captae et excīsae sunt.*
142. **ipsōs** = *eōs.*
     prīmum . . . mox etiam – *first . . . [and] soon also.*
     aciē – *in battle.*
143. **obsidēns** – *besieging.*
     dītissimam – *wealthiest.*
144. **et** = *etiam.*
     nōbilem – *famous.*
     eī – *against him.*
145. **invidia** – *ill will.*
     quasi – *on the grounds that.*
     praedam – *spoils.*
     damnātusque . . . expulsus = *damnātusque est . . . expulsus est.*

that victim would be given the victory, and were moved to open the mine and seize the entrails, which they bore off to the dictator.

Livy, *Ab urbe condita* 5.21

Sack of Rome by the Gauls, 390 BCE

Statim Gallī Senonēs ad urbem vēnērunt et victōs Rōmānōs ūndecimō mīliāriō ā Rōmā apud flūmen Alliam secūtī etiam urbem occupāvērunt. Neque dēfendī quicquam nisi Capitōlium potuit; quod cum diū obsē- dissent et iam Rōmānī famē labōrārent, acceptō aurō nē Capitōlium ob-   150 sidērent, recessērunt.

> *VAE VICTIS!*
>
> Day after day [the Romans] looked out to see if any relief from the dictator was at hand; but at last even hope, as well as food, begin- ning to fail them, and their bodies growing almost too weak to sus- tain their armour when they went out on picket duty, they declared that they must either surrender or ransom themselves, on whatever conditions they could make; for the Gauls were hinting very plainly that no great price would be required to induce them to raise the siege. Thereupon the senate met, and instructed the tribunes of the soldiers to arrange the terms. Then, at a conference between Quintus Sulpicius the tribune and the Gallic chieftain Brennus, the affair was settled, and a thousand pounds of gold was agreed on as the price of a people that was destined presently to rule the na-

continued

147. **victōs Rōmānōs . . . secūtī** – *having followed the defeated Romans.*
    ūndecimō – *eleventh.*
149. **Neque dēfendī quicquam . . . potuit** – *nor was anything able to be defended.*
    nisi – *except.*
    quod = *et id.*
    obsēdissent – *had besieged.*

tions. The transaction was a foul disgrace in itself, but an insult was added thereto: the weights brought by the Gauls were dishonest, and on the tribune's objecting, the insolent Gaul added his sword to the weight, and a saying intolerable to Roman ears was heard— Woe to the conquered!

Livy, *Ab urbe condita* 5.48

Sed ā Camillō, quī in vīcīnā cīvitāte exulābat, Gallīs superventum est gravissiméque victī sunt. Posteā tamen etiam secūtus eōs Camillus ita cecīdit ut et aurum, quod hīs datum fuerat, et omnia, quae cēperant, 155 mīlitāria signa revocāret. Ita tertiō triumphāns urbem ingressus est et appellātus secundus Rōmulus, quasi et ipse patriae conditor.

A ROMULUS AND FATHER OF HIS COUNTRY AND A
SECOND FOUNDER OF THE CITY

But neither gods nor men would suffer the Romans to live ransomed. For, by some chance, before the infamous payment had

152. **ā Camillō . . . Gallīs superventum est** – *it was come upon for the Gauls unexpectedly by Camillus = the Gauls were come upon unexpectedly by Camillus.*
exulābat – *was in exile.*

153. **victī sunt** = *Gallī victī sunt.*
secūtus eōs Camillus – *Camillus having followed them.*

154. **cecīdit** – *slaughtered [them].*
et . . . et – *both . . . and.*
datum fuerat = *datum erat.*
omnia . . . mīlitāria signa – *all the military standards.*

155. **tertiō** – *for the third time.*
triumphāns – *in a triumphal procession.*
appellātus = *appellātus est.*

156. **quasi . . . conditor** = *quasi . . . conditor esset.*
et = *etiam.*

been consummated, and when the gold had not yet, owing to the dispute, been all weighed out, the dictator appeared and commanded the gold to be cleared away and the Gauls to leave. They objected vehemently, and insisted on the compact; but Camillus denied the validity of that compact which, subsequently to his own appointment as dictator, an inferior magistrate had made without his authorization, and warned them to prepare for battle. His own men he ordered to throw their packs in a heap, make ready their weapons, and win their country back with iron instead of gold; having before their eyes the temples of the gods, their wives and their children, the soil of their native land, with the hideous marks of war upon it, and all that religion called upon them to defend, recover, or avenge. He then drew up his line, as well as the ground permitted, on the naturally uneven surface of the half-ruined City, and saw to it that his soldiers had every advantage in choice of position and in preparation which the art of war suggested. The Gauls were taken aback; they armed, and, with more rage than judgment, charged the Romans. But now fortune had turned; now the might of Heaven and human wisdom were engaged in the cause of Rome. Accordingly, at the first shock the Gauls were routed with as little effort as they had themselves put forth to conquer on the Allia. They afterwards fought a second, more regular engagement, eight miles out on the Gabinian Way, where they had rallied from their flight, and again the generalship and auspices of Camillus overcame them. Here the carnage was universal; their camp was taken; and not a man survived to tell of the disaster. The dictator, having recovered his country from her enemies, returned in triumph to the city; and between the rough jests uttered by the soldiers, was hailed in no unmeaning terms of praise as a Romulus and Father of his Country and a second Founder of the City.

Livy, *Ab urbe condita* 5.49

Lupa capitolina. Wolf, 12th–13th century; twins, 15th century. Bronze. Capitoline Museums, Rome. Photo by Jean-Pol Grandmont, via Wikimedia Commons.

Unannotated Latin Text

This section of bare Latin text has been included for use during classroom translation. Not having the notes under one's eye in the classroom ensures that the glosses are not used as a crutch and that grammatical concepts have been thoroughly learned. This section is intended for use only after the corresponding passages in the Text and Notes section have been read.

Romulus and the foundation of Rome, 753–715 BCE

I. Rōmānum imperium ā Rōmulō exōrdium habet, quī Rēae Silviae, Vestālis virginis, fīlius et, quantum putātus est, Mārtis cum Remō frātre ūnō partū ēditus est. Is, cum inter pāstōrēs latrōcinārētur, decem et octō annōs nātus urbem exiguam in Palātīnō monte cōnstituit XI Kal. Maiās, Olympiadis sextae annō tertiō, post Trōiae excidium, ut quī plūrimum minimumque trādunt, annō trecentēsimō nōnāgēsimō quārtō. 5

II. Conditā cīvitāte, quam ex nōmine suō Rōmam vocāvit, haec ferē ēgit: multitūdinem fīnitimōrum in cīvitātem recēpit, centum ex seniōribus lēgit, quōrum cōnsiliō omnia ageret, quōs senātōrēs nōmināvit propter senectūtem. Tum, cum uxōrēs ipse et populus suus nōn habērent, invītāvit 10 ad spectāculum lūdōrum vīcīnās urbī Rōmae nātiōnēs atque eārum virginēs rapuit. Commōtīs bellīs propter raptārum iniūriam Caenīnēnsēs vīcit, Antemnātēs, Crustumīnōs, Sabīnōs, Fīdēnātēs, Vēientēs. Haec omnia oppida urbem cingunt.

Et cum, ortā subitō tempestāte, nōn compāruisset, annō rēgnī trīcēsimō 15 septimō ad deōs trānsīsse crēditus est et cōnsecrātus. Deinde Rōmae per

quīnōs diēs senātōrēs imperāvērunt et hīs rēgnantibus annus ūnus complētus est.

Numa Pompilius, 715–672 BCE

III. Posteā Numa Pompilius rēx creātus est, quī bellum quidem nūl-
20 lum gessit, sed nōn minus cīvitātī quam Rōmulus prōfuit. Nam et lēgēs
Rōmānīs mōrēsque cōnstituit, quī cōnsuētūdine proeliōrum iam latrōnēs
ac sēmibarbarī putābantur, et annum dēscrīpsit in decem mēnsēs prius
sine aliquā supputātiōne cōnfūsum, et īnfīnīta Rōmae sacra ac templa
cōnstituit. Morbō dēcessit quadrāgēsimō et tertiō imperiī annō.

Tullus Hostilius, 672–642 BCE

25 IV. Huic successit Tullus Hostīlius. Hic bella reparāvit, Albānōs vīcit, quī
ab urbe Rōmā duodecimō mīliāriō sunt, Vēientēs et Fīdēnātēs, quōrum
aliī sextō mīliāriō absunt ab urbe Rōmā, aliī octāvō decimō, bellō superāvit, urbem ampliāvit, adiectō Caeliō monte. Cum trīgintā et duōs
annōs rēgnāsset, fulmine ictus cum domō suā ārsit.

Ancus Marcius, 642–616 BCE

30 V. Post hunc Ancus Mārcius, Numae ex fīliā nepōs, suscēpit imperium.
Contrā Latīnōs dīmicāvit, Aventīnum montem cīvitātī adiēcit et Iāniculum, apud ōstium Tiberis cīvitātem suprā mare sextō decimō mīliāriō ab
urbe Rōmā condidit. Vīcēsimō et quārtō annō imperiī morbō periit.

Tarquinius Priscus, 616–578 BCE

VI. Deinde rēgnum Prīscus Tarquinius accēpit. Hic numerum senātōrum
35 duplicāvit, circum Rōmae aedificāvit, lūdōs Rōmānōs īnstituit, quī ad
nostram memoriam permanent. Vīcit īdem etiam Sabīnōs et nōn parum

agrōrum sublātum īsdem urbis Rōmae territōriō iūnxit, prīmusque triumphāns urbem intrāvit. Mūrōs fēcit et cloācās, Capitōlium inchoāvit.
Trīcēsimō octāvō imperiī annō per Ancī fīliōs occīsus est, rēgis eius cuī
ipse successerat.   40

Servius Tullius, 579–534 BCE

VII. Post hunc Servius Tullius suscēpit imperium, genitus ex nōbilī
fēminā, captīvā tamen et ancillā. Hic quoque Sabīnōs subēgit, montēs
trēs, Quirīnālem, Vīminālem, Ēsquilīnum, urbī adiūnxit, fossās circum
mūrum dūxit. Prīmus omnium cēnsum ōrdināvit, quī adhūc per orbem
terrārum incognitus erat. Sub eō, Rōma, omnibus in cēnsum dēlātīs,   45
habuit capita LXXXIII mīlia cīvium Rōmānōrum cum hīs quī in agrīs
erant. Occīsus est scelere generī suī Tarquiniī Superbī, fīliī eius rēgis, cuī
ipse successerat, et fīliae, quam Tarquinius habēbat uxōrem.

Tarquinius Superbus, 534–510 BCE

VIII. L. Tarquinius Superbus, septimus atque ultimus rēgum, Volscōs,
quae gēns ad Campāniam euntibus nōn longē ab urbe est, vīcit, Gabiōs   50
cīvitātem et Suessam Pōmētiam subēgit, cum Tuscīs pācem fēcit et templum Iovis in Capitōliō aedificāvit. Posteā, Ardeam oppugnāns, in octāvō
decimō mīliāriō ab urbe Rōmā positam cīvitātem, imperium perdidit.
Nam cum fīlius eius, et ipse Tarquinius iūnior, nōbilissimam fēminam
Lucrētiam eandemque pudīcissimam, Collātīnī uxōrem, stuprāsset eaque   55
dē iniūriā marītō et patrī et amīcīs questa fuisset, in omnium cōnspectū
sē occīdit. Propter quam causam Brūtus, parēns et ipse Tarquiniī, populum concitāvit et Tarquiniō adēmit imperium. Mox exercitus quoque eum,
quī cīvitātem Ardeam cum ipsō rēge oppugnābat, relīquit; veniēnsque ad
urbem rēx, portīs clausīs, exclūsus est, cumque imperāsset annōs quat-   60
tuor et vīgintī cum uxōre et līberīs suīs fūgit. Ita Rōmae rēgnātum est per
septem rēgēs annīs ducentīs quadrāgintā tribus, cum adhūc Rōma, ubi
plūrimum, vix ūsque ad quīntum decimum mīliārium possidēret.

Founding of the Republic, 509 BCE

IX. Hinc cōnsulēs coepēre, prō ūnō rēge duo, hāc causā creātī, ut, sī ūnus
65 malus esse voluisset, alter eum, habēns potestātem similem, coercēret. Et
placuit, nē imperium longius quam annuum habērent, nē per diūturnitātem potestātis īnsolentiōrēs redderentur, sed cīvīlēs semper essent, quī
sē post annum scīrent futūrōs esse prīvātōs. Fuērunt igitur, annō prīmō
expulsīs rēgibus, cōnsulēs L. Iūnius Brūtus, quī maximē ēgerat ut Tarqui-
70 nius pellerētur, et Tarquinius Collātīnus, marītus Lucrētiae. Sed Tarquiniō
Collātīnō statim sublāta est dignitās. Placuerat enim, nē quisquam in urbe
remanēret quī Tarquinius vocārētur. Ergō, acceptō omnī patrimōniō suō,
ex urbe migrāvit, et locō ipsīus factus est L. Valerius Pūblicola cōnsul.
Commōvit tamen bellum urbī Rōmae rēx Tarquinius, quī fuerat expulsus,
75 et collēctīs multīs gentibus, ut in rēgnum posset restituī dīmicāvit.

War with Tarquinius Superbus, 509 BCE

X. In prīmā pugnā Brūtus cōnsul et Arrūns, Tarquiniī fīlius, in vicem
sē occīdērunt, Rōmānī tamen ex eā pugnā victōrēs recessērunt. Brūtum
mātrōnae Rōmānae, dēfēnsōrem pudīcitiae suae, quasi commūnem patrem per annum lūxērunt. Valerius Pūblicola Sp. Lucrētium Tricipitīnum
80 collēgam sibi fēcit, Lucrētiae patrem, quō morbō mortuō iterum Horātium Pulvillum collēgam sibi sūmpsit. Ita prīmus annus quīnque cōnsulēs habuit, cum Tarquinius Collātīnus propter nōmen urbe cessisset,
Brūtus in proeliō perīsset, Sp. Lucrētius morbō mortuus esset.

War with Lars Porsenna, 508 BCE

XI. Secundō quoque annō iterum Tarquinius, ut reciperētur in rēgnum,
85 bellum Rōmānīs intulit, auxilium eī ferente Porsennā, Tusciae rēge, et
Rōmam paene cēpit. Vērum tum quoque victus est. Tertiō annō post rēgēs
exāctōs, Tarquinius, cum suscipī nōn posset in rēgnum neque eī Porsenna, quī pācem cum Rōmānīs fēcerat, praestāret auxilium, Tusculum sē

contulit, quae cīvitās nōn longē ab urbe est, atque ibi per quattuordecim
annōs prīvātus cum uxōre cōnsenuit.   90

Quārtō annō post rēgēs exāctōs, cum Sabīnī Rōmānīs bellum intulissent,
victī sunt et dē hīs triumphātum est. Quīntō annō L. Valerius ille, Brūtī
collēga et quater cōnsul, fātāliter mortuus est, adeō pauper ut, collātīs ā
populō nummīs, sūmptum habuerit sepultūrae. Quem mātrōnae sīcutī
Brūtum annum lūxērunt.   95

The Dictatorship, 501 BCE

XII. Nōnō annō post rēgēs exāctōs, cum gener Tarquiniī ad iniūriam socerī vindicandam ingentem collēgisset exercitum, nova Rōmae dignitās
est creāta, quae dictātūra appellātur, maior quam cōnsulātus. Eōdem annō
etiam magister equitum factus est, quī dictātōrī obsequerētur. Dictātor
autem Rōmae prīmus fuit T. Larcius, magister equitum prīmus Sp. Cassius.   100

Secession of the Plebeians, 494 BCE

XIII. Sextō decimō annō post rēgēs exāctōs, sēditiōnem populus Rōmae
fēcit, tamquam ā senātū atque cōnsulibus premerētur. Tum et ipse sibi
tribūnōs plēbis quasi propriōs iūdicēs et dēfēnsōrēs creāvit, per quōs contrā senātum et cōnsulēs tūtus esse posset.

War with the Volsci, 493 BCE

XIV. Sequentī annō Volscī contrā Rōmānōs bellum reparāvērunt, et victī   105
aciē etiam Coriolōs cīvitātem, quam habēbant optimam, perdidērunt.

Coriolanus, 491 BCE

XV. Octāvō decimō annō postquam rēgēs ēiectī erant, expulsus ex urbe
Q. Mārcius, dux Rōmānus, quī Coriolōs cēperat, Volscōrum cīvitātem, ad
ipsōs Volscōs contendit īrātus et auxilia contrā Rōmānōs accēpit. Rōmānōs

110 saepe vīcit, ūsque ad quīntum mīliārium urbis accessit, oppugnātūrus etiam patriam suam, lēgātīs quī pācem petēbant repudiātīs, nisi ad eum māter Veturia et uxor Volumnia ex urbe vēnissent, quārum flētū et dēprecātiōne superātus remōvit exercitum. Atque hic secundus post Tarquinium fuit, quī dux contrā patriam suam esset.

Disaster at Cremera, 479 BCE

115 XVI. C. Fabiō et L. Virgīniō cōnsulibus, trecentī nōbilēs hominēs, quī ex Fabiā familiā erant, contrā Vēientēs bellum sōlī suscēpērunt, prōmittentēs senātuī et populō per sē omne certāmen implendum. Itaque profectī, omnēs nōbilēs et quī singulī magnōrum exercituum ducēs esse dēbērent, in proeliō concidērunt. Ūnus omnīnō superfuit ex tantā familiā, quī prop-

120 ter aetātem puerīlem dūcī nōn potuerat ad pugnam. Post haec cēnsus in urbe habitus est et inventa sunt cīvium capita CXVII mīlia CCCXIX.

Cincinnatus, 458 BCE

XVII. Sequentī annō cum in Algidō monte ab urbe duodecimō fermē mīliāriō Rōmānus obsidērētur exercitus, L. Quīntius Cincinnātus dictātor est factus, quī agrum quattuor iūgerum possidēns manibus suīs colēbat.

125 Is cum in opere et arāns esset inventus, sūdōre dētersō togam praetextam accēpit et caesīs hostibus līberāvit exercitum.

The Decemviri, 451–449 BCE

XVIII. Annō trecentēsimō et alterō ab urbe conditā imperium cōnsulāre cessāvit et prō duōbus cōnsulibus decem factī sunt, quī summam potestātem habērent, decemvirī nōminātī. Sed cum prīmō annō bene

130 ēgissent, secundō ūnus ex hīs, Ap. Claudius, Virgīniī cuiusdam, quī honestīs iam stīpendiīs contrā Latīnōs in monte Algidō mīlitārat, fīliam virginem corrumpere voluit; quam pater occīdit, nē stuprum ā decemvirō sustinēret, et regressus ad mīlitēs mōvit tumultum. Sublāta est decemvirīs potestās ipsīque damnātī sunt.

Gavin Hamilton, *The Death of Lucretia*, 1763–67. Oil on canvas. Yale Center for British Art, Paul Mellon Collection, via Wikimedia Commons.

Revolt of Fidenae, 438 BCE

XIX. Annō trecentēsimō et quīntō decimō ab urbe conditā Fīdēnātēs con- 135
trā Rōmānōs rebellāvērunt. Auxilium hīs praestābant Vēientēs et rēx Vēien-
tium Tolumnius. Quae ambae cīvitātēs tam vīcīnae urbī sunt ut Fīdēnae
sextō, Vēī octāvō decimō mīliāriō absint. Coniūnxērunt sē hīs et Volscī.
Sed Mam. Aemiliō dictātōre et L. Quīntiō Cincinnātō magistrō equitum,
victī etiam rēgem perdidērunt. Fīdēnae captae et excīsae. 140

War with Veii, 396 BCE

XX. Post vīgintī deinde annōs Vēientānī rebellāvērunt. Dictātor contrā
ipsōs missus est Fūrius Camillus, quī prīmum eōs vīcit aciē, mox etiam

cīvitātem diū obsidēns cēpit, antīquissimam Ītaliaeque dītissimam. Post
eam, cēpit et Faliscōs, nōn minus nōbilem cīvitātem. Sed commōta est eī
145   invidia, quasi praedam male dīvīsisset, damnātusque ob eam causam et
expulsus cīvitāte.

Sack of Rome by the Gauls, 390 BCE

Statim Gallī Senonēs ad urbem vēnērunt et victōs Rōmānōs ūndecimō
mīliāriō ā Rōmā apud flūmen Alliam secūtī etiam urbem occupāvērunt.
Neque dēfendī quicquam nisi Capitōlium potuit; quod cum diū obsē-
150   dissent et iam Rōmānī famē labōrārent, acceptō aurō nē Capitōlium obsidērent, recessērunt.

Sed ā Camillō, quī in vīcīnā cīvitāte exulābat, Gallīs superventum est
gravissiméque victī sunt. Posteā tamen etiam secūtus eōs Camillus ita
cecīdit ut et aurum, quod hīs datum fuerat, et omnia, quae cēperant,
155   mīlitāria signa revocāret. Ita tertiō triumphāns urbem ingressus est et appellātus secundus Rōmulus, quasi et ipse patriae conditor.

COMMENTARY

This section contains a running commentary on the grammar and syntax of Book I of the *Breviarium*, as well as historical background on the Roman Regal period and early Republic (historical notes are set off in boxes, for easy reference). The running commentary need not be read in its entirety but may be referred to on an as-needed basis. Abbreviated cross-references are included for the following commonly used textbooks (those marked with an asterisk may be found in Appendix B: Additional Textbook Cross-References):

A&G   *Allen and Greenough's New Latin Grammar* (New Rochelle, NY: Aristide D. Caratzas, 1983) [reprint of 1903 edition]. Available online from the Perseus Digital Library at www.perseus.tufts.edu.

CLC   *Cambridge Latin Course: Unit 3*, 4th Edition (New York: Cambridge University Press, 2002).

ER   *Ecce Romani II*, 4th Edition (Upper Saddle River, NJ: Prentice Hall, 2009).

J*   *Jenney's Second Year Latin* (Upper Saddle River, NJ: Prentice Hall, 1990).

LFA   *Latin for Americans*, Level 2 (New York: Glencoe/McGraw-Hill, 2004).

LFNM   *Latin for the New Millennium*, Level 2 (Mundelein, IL: Bolchazy-Carducci, 2009).

LTRL*   *Learn to Read Latin*, by Andrew Keller and Stephanie Russell (New Haven: Yale University Press, 2003).

M&F*   *Latin: An Intensive Course*, by Floyd L. Moreland and Rita M. Fleischer (Berkeley: University of California Press, 1977).

OLC*   *Oxford Latin Course, Part III*, 2nd Edition (New York: Oxford
        University Press, 1997).
W   *Wheelock's Latin*, 7th Edition, Revised (New York: Harper Collins,
        2011).

Chapter I

1. **Rōmānum imperium** – A slightly more expected word order would
   be *imperium Rōmānum;* the emphatic word order makes *Rōmānum*
   the first word of the entire work. *Imperium* may here be translated as
   empire; its basic meaning is *power* or *authority to command.*

Rōmulō . . . Remō frātre – Romulus and Remus are the twin brothers
central to Rome's foundation legend. The name *Romulus* is a back-for-
mation from the name of the city itself, and simply means *Roman.*
Remus may be an alternate version of the same name, later misunder-
stood to be a different person and incorporated into the narrative.

Rēae Silviae, Vestālis virginis – genitives modifying *fīlius.*

2. **fīlius** – in apposition to *quī* (W 25, LFA 8, A&G §282).

   quantum putātus est – *as he was thought.* This wording is used to distance
   the author from the supernatural elements of the narrative. **putātus est**
   – perfect passive of *putō, -āre;* note that the masculine ending indicates
   the *personal construction* (the subject is *he*, not the impersonal *it*) (A&G
   §582).

   ūnō partū – *ablative of manner* (W 116–17, ER 347, CLC 326–27, A&G
   §412).

3. **ēditus est** – perfect passive of *ēdō, -ere.*

Vestālis virginis – The Vestal Virgins were attendants to the Roman
hearth goddess, Vesta. The cult of Vesta was one of the oldest and
most important at Rome.

Is, cum inter pāstōrēs latrōcinārētur, . . . urbem exiguam in Palātīnō monte cōnstituit – The version of the story given by the Roman historian Livy (whose work, in an epitomized form, was Eutropius's main source for this period) is as follows. Numitor, the king of Alba Longa, a small city near Rome founded by Aeneas's son Ascanius, was deposed by his brother Amulius. To prevent the birth of potential rivals to the throne, Amulius made Numitor's daughter, Rea Silvia, a Vestal Virgin. Rea, however, was raped by Mars and gave birth to twins. On the king's orders, the twins were thrown into the Tiber River. A passing female wolf—an animal sacred to Mars— heard the babies' cries and nursed them until they were discovered by the shepherd Faustulus. The boys were raised by Faustulus and distinguished themselves in strength and courage. They developed a following of young men by attacking brigands and distributing the plunder among the local shepherds. After learning their true identity, Romulus and Remus restored the rightful king Numitor to his throne. The twins then decided to found their own city on the site of the Tiber where they had been abandoned as babies.

cum inter pāstōrēs latrōcinārētur – *cum clause (circumstantial)* (W 255– 56, ER 361, LFA 504, CLC 70, LFNM 260–61, A&G §546); *latrōcinārētur* is an imperfect subjunctive of the deponent verb *latrōcinor, -ārī*. It is usually best to translate the subjunctive in a *cum clause* as the indicative of the corresponding tense (e.g., translate *latrōcinārētur* as *latrōcinābātur*, *was leading the life of a bandit*).

decem et octō annōs nātus – The Romans counted the birth year and the current year inclusively, so *having been born eighteen years* would be *at seventeen years of age* in a noninclusive counting. **nātus** – perfect participle of the deponent verb *nāscor, nāscī*.

4. Palātīnō monte – Archeological evidence supports the primacy of the Palatine in the very early history of the city, and the eighth cen-

continued

tury BCE as the date of the earliest settlements there. For locations of the seven hills of Rome, see Appendix A: Maps.

XI Kal. Maiās – The date April 21 coincided with the Parilia, the festival in honor of the shepherd deity Pales. This was one of the oldest religious festivals at Rome.

Olympiadis sextae annō tertiō – The Greek Olympiad was a four-year period reckoned from each Olympic game. The first Olympic game was held in 776 BCE, making the third year of the sixth Olympiad either 754 or 753 BCE, depending on the method of calculation used.

Olympiadis – genitive modifying *annō tertiō*.

5. **annō tertiō** and **annō trecentēsimō nōnāgēsimō quārtō** – *ablative of time when* (no preposition is used) (W 125, ER 346, LFA 7, LFNM 496, CLC 326–27, A&G §423).

post Trōiae excidium . . . annō trecentēsimō nōnāgēsimō quārtō – The English word order would be *annō trecentēsimō nōnāgēsimō quārtō post excidium Trōiae*.

---

post Trōiae excidium – The reference to the fall of Troy alludes to the tradition that the Trojan prince Aeneas was the progenitor of the Romans. This tradition is thought to have become current at a later date than that of the Romulus legend (that is, after contact with Greeks from Asia Minor or Sicily). Originally, the two stories were mutually exclusive: the traditional dates for the fall of Troy and the foundation of Rome are separated by some four hundred years. Later historians synthesized the two stories by having Aeneas's son found Alba Longa, a small city near Rome, and inserting a reign of twelve Alban kings.

---

6. **annō trecentēsimō nōnāgēsimō quārtō** – The date that Eutropius gives here for the fall of Troy, 1148 BCE, is slightly later than the more widely used date given by the Greek mathematician Eratosthenes, 1183 BCE.

Chapter II

7. **Conditā cīvitāte** – *ablative absolute* (W 193–94, ER 348, LFA 33, LFNM 298–99, CLC 218, A&G §419). It usually makes better English to translate the ablative absolute as a subordinate clause and choose an appropriate conjunction such as *when, since, although,* or *after* (e.g., *after the city had been founded* instead of the more literal *with the city having been founded*). The active voice also makes slightly better English, even though the Latin is passive. **Conditā** – perfect passive participle of *condō, -ere*. **cīvitāte** – Eutropius uses *cīvitās* as a synonym for *urbs, city*. This is a late usage (in classical Latin, *cīvitās* means *state* or *citizenship*). Notice that the word for *city* in many of the Romance languages comes from this late usage: *città, ciudad, cidade, cité*.

   quam – The antecedent is *cīvitāte*.

   haec – plural *substantive* (W 27, ER 349, LFNM 475, A&G §288) from *hic, haec, hoc*; translate here as *this*, rather than the more literal *these things*.

   ēgit – perfect of *agō, -ere*.

8. **multitūdinem finitimōrum in cīvitātem recēpit, centum ex seniōribus lēgit** – The omission of a conjunction between clauses is called *asyndeton*. **finitimōrum** – *partitive genitive* (W 124, ER 342, LFA 25, CLC 324, A&G §346). **centum ex seniōribus** – *Ex* or *dē* with the ablative is often used with cardinal numbers (literally *one hundred from the elders*) (W 125, ER 342, A&G §346c). Compare this construction to the *partitive genitive, finitimōrum*, in the previous clause.

> **centum ex seniōribus . . . quōs senātōrēs nōmināvit** – The senate
> was an advisory body that originated in the Regal period and contin-
> ued through the Republic and the Empire. Eutropius's account of
> an original senate of one hundred members is traditional. For the
> increase in the number of senators during the later Regal period,
> see the note for *numerum senātōrum duplicāvit*, line 34.

9. **quōrum cōnsiliō omnia ageret** – *purpose clause* introduced by the
   relative pronoun (W 328, LFNM 509, CLC 179, A&G §531.2). As in *ut-
   purpose clauses*, the imperfect subjunctive may be rendered with the
   English auxiliary *might* (*by whose advice he might manage all things*) or
   with the English infinitive (*to manage all things by their advice*). **cōnsiliō**
   – *ablative of means or instrument* (W 116, ER 346, LFA 20, LFNM 486,
   CLC 326–27, A&G §409). **omnia** – plural *substantive* (W 35, ER 349,
   A&G §288) from *omnis, omne*.

10. **cum . . . nōn habērent** – *cum clause (causal)* (W 255–56, ER 361, LFA
    504, LFNM 265, A&G §549). Render *cum* in this clause as *since*.

    uxōrēs – object of *habērent*.

> 11. **vīcīnās urbī Rōmae nātiōnēs** – The neighbors here are the Sa-
> bines, a central Apennine people who also inhabited Latium dur-
> ing Rome's early history (see Appendix A: Maps). According to the
> Roman historical tradition, after peace was established between the
> two peoples, the Romans and the Sabines formed a single state,
> with their kings—Romulus and Titus Tatius—ruling jointly. Lin-
> guistic and archeological evidence supports a very early Sabine ele-
> ment in Roman culture.

   vīcīnās urbī Rōmae nātiōnēs – *vīcīnās* modifies *nātiōnēs; urbī Rōmae* is
   dative with *vīcīnās* (A&G §384).

   eārum – The antecedent is *nātiōnēs*.

12. **Commōtīs bellīs** – *ablative absolute* (W 193–94, ER 348, LFA 33, LFNM

298–99, CLC 218, A&G §419). **Commōtīs** – perfect passive participle of *commoveō, -ēre.*

Caenīnēnsēs vīcit, Antemnātēs, Crustumīnōs, Sabīnōs, Fīdēnātēs, Vēientēs – Caenina, Antemnae, and Crustumerium were communities absorbed by Rome early in her history. Veii was Rome's nearest Etruscan neighbor, and Fidenae, five miles north of Rome on the Tiber, was Veii's stronghold (see Appendix A: Maps). These cities were to become vexing enemies to Rome in the fifth century BCE (see Chapters XVI, XIX, and XX). The tradition that Rome was engaged in conflict with Veii and Fidenae during the eighth century is not historical and perhaps arose to establish a precedent from the reign of Romulus for the later, historical struggles.

Caenīnēnsēs . . . Antemnātēs, Crustumīnōs, Sabīnōs, Fīdēnātēs, Vēientēs – objects of *vīcit.* **vīcit** – perfect of *vincō, -ere.*

13. **Haec omnia oppida urbem cingunt** – *Haec omnia oppida* is the subject and *urbem* the direct object of *cingunt.*

15. **cum . . . nōn compāruisset** – *cum clause (circumstantial)* (W 255–56, ER 361, LFA 504, LFNM 260–61, CLC 70, A&G §546). Render *cum* into English here as *when. Compāruisset* is the pluperfect subjunctive of *compāreō, -ēre;* translate here with the corresponding indicative (*he had not appeared*).

   ortā . . . tempestāte – *ablative absolute* (W 193–94, ER 348, LFA 33, LFNM 298–99, CLC 218, A&G §419); *ortā* is the perfect participle of the deponent verb *orior, -īrī.*

   annō . . . trīcēsimō septimō – *ablative of time when* (no preposition is used) (W 125, ER 346, LFA 7, LFNM 496, CLC 326–27, A&G §423). **rēgnī** – genitive singular.

---

16. **ad deōs trānsīsse crēditus est** – The tradition about the death of Romulus is contradictory. The Roman historian Livy records the suspicion that he was murdered by the senators.

---

trānsīsse – perfect infinitive of *trānseō, -īre.*

crēditus est – perfect passive of *crēdō, -ere.*

cōnsecrātus [est] – perfect passive of *cōnsecrō, -āre.*

Deinde Rōmae per quīnōs diēs senātōrēs imperāvērunt – The tenure of power between the reigns of kings is called an interregnum. This institution was retained in the Republic and used at the death or resignation of both consuls.

Rōmae – *locative* (W 314, ER 349, LFA 178, LFNM 26–28, CLC 327, A&G §427): *at Rome.*

per quīnōs diēs – *accusative of duration of time (per is sometimes used for emphasis)* (W 314, LFNM 495, CLC 149, A&G §424a). **quīnōs** – *distributive numeral, five each, five apiece, etc.* (W 130, LFNM 497, A&G §136–37).

17. **hīs rēgnantibus** – *ablative absolute* (W 193–94, ER 348, LFA 33, LFNM 298–99, CLC 218, A&G §419).

complētus est – perfect passive of *compleō, -ēre.*

Chapter III

---

19. **Numa Pompilius** – The name *Numa Pompilius* may be of Sabine origin, further evidence of an early Sabine influence at Rome. Numa is the priestly counterpart to Romulus: while Romulus is the archetype of the warrior-king, Numa is the archetype of the priest-king. The religious innovations that the Roman tradition attributes to Numa, however, actually belong to a later, Etruscan period.

---

creātus est – perfect passive of *creō, -āre.*

quidem – Note that this is *quidem (indeed)*, not *quīdam (a certain).*

20. **gessit** – perfect of *gerō, -ere.*

cīvitātī – *dative with a compound verb, prōfuit* (W 296, ER 343, LFA 173, CLC 325, A&G §370).

prōfuit – perfect of *prōsum, -desse.*

et . . . cōnstituit . . . et . . . dēscrīpsit . . . et . . . cōnstituit – Note that the three main clauses are each introduced by the conjunction *et.*

21. **Rōmānīs** – *dative of indirect object.*

quī – The antecedent is *Rōmānīs.*

cōnsuētūdine – *ablative of cause* (W 493, ER 346, LFA 499, LFNM 495, A&G §404). This construction is sometimes difficult to distinguish from the *ablative of means or instrument* (W 116–17, ER 346, LFA 20, LFNM 486, CLC 326–27, A&G §409).

latrōnēs ac sēmibarbarī – *predicate nominative* (W 34, ER 341, LFNM 473, CLC 324, A&G §283).

22. **putābantur** – *inceptive imperfect* (A&G §471c): *began to be thought.*

> **annum dēscrīpsit in decem mēnsēs** – Both the Roman historian Livy and the Greek historian Plutarch say that Numa fixed the calendar at twelve months, not ten, as Eutropius claims. According to this tradition, Numa added January and February to the earlier, ten-month calendar (which may have had an uncounted gap in the winter). The change to a twelve-month calendar, however, more likely belongs to the Etruscan period, a century later.

23. **cōnfūsum** – perfect passive participle of *cōnfundō, -ere;* modifies *annum.*

Rōmae – *locative* (W 314, ER 349, LFA 178, LFNM 26–28, CLC 327, A&G §427): *at Rome.*

sacra – plural *substantive* (W 35, ER 349, LFNM 475, A&G §288) from *sacer, sacra, sacrum.* Render into English as *sacred rites, observances,* or *ceremonies.*

24. **Morbō** – *ablative of cause* (W 493, ER 346, LFA 499, LFNM 495, A&G §404).

    dēcessit – perfect of *dēcēdō, -ere*.

    quadrāgēsimō et tertiō . . . annō – *ablative of time when* (no preposition is used) (W 125, ER 346, LFA 7, LFNM 496, CLC 326–27, A&G §423).

Chapter IV

25. **Huic** – *dative with a compound verb* (W 296, ER 343, LFA 173, CLC 325, A&G §370). Translate as if this were the direct object of *successit*.

    successit – perfect of *succēdō, -ere*.

Tullus Hostīlius – While Tullus Hostilius's reign is characterized primarily by legendary military exploits, his name is most likely that of a historical person: Tullus is an authentic Latin or Volscian praenomen, and the name *Hostilius* was associated with the original senate house, the Curia Hostilia, long before the gens Hostilia came into prominence. The fact that the Hostilii were a plebeian family also makes it less likely that the name is a later invention. The tradition of Tullus's military exploits may have arisen to explain the gens name (which means *hostile*) and to emphasize the contrast between him and his priestly predecessor, Numa.

Hic bella reparāvit . . . urbem ampliāvit, adiectō Caeliō monte – *Hic* governs four verbs, each with a direct object: *bella reparāvit; Albānōs vīcit; Vēientēs et Fīdēnātēs superāvit; urbem ampliāvit*. The English word order would be *Hic reparāvit bella, vīcit Albānōs (quī sunt duodecimō mīliāriō ab urbe Rōmā), superāvit bellō Vēientēs et Fīdēnātēs (aliī quōrum absunt ab urbe Rōmā sextō mīliāriō, aliī octāvō decimō), ampliāvit urbem, Caeliō monte adiectō.*

> **Albānōs vīcit** – Alba Longa was the ancient Latin city said to have
> been founded by Aeneas's son Ascanius. It was the early leader of a
> confederation of Latin cities (see note on *Contrā Latīnōs dīmicāvit*,
> line 31). The capture of Alba by Rome in the seventh century BCE is
> probably historical.

26. **duodecimō mīliāriō** – *ablative of place where* (W 177, ER 344, LFA 7,
    LFNM 477, CLC 326–27, A&G §426): *at the twelfth mile marker*. The
    preposition *in* is often omitted when an adjective modifies the noun
    (LFA 7, A&G §429.2). The same construction is used at lines 27, 32,
    52, 122, 138, and 147.

> **mīliāriō** – Milestones were set up at intervals of one thousand paces
> (*milia passuum*). This was equivalent to 4,854 feet, slightly shorter
> than the modern mile. Throughout Book I, Eutropius provides dis-
> tances from Rome for many of the places he mentions. This infor-
> mation does not come from his principal source, an Epitome of Livy.

27. **bellō** – *ablative of time when* (no preposition is used) (W 125, ER 346,
    LFA 7, CLC 326–27, A&G §423). Many expressions use the construction
    time when where in English the main idea is *place* (A&G §424d).

28. **adiectō Caeliō monte** – *ablative absolute* (W 193–94, ER 348, LFA 33,
    LFNM 298–99, CLC 218, A&G §419). For the location of the seven hills
    of Rome, see Appendix A: Maps. **adiectō** – perfect passive participle of
    adiciō, -ere.

    Cum . . . rēgnāsset – *cum clause (circumstantial)* (W 255–56, ER 361, LFA
    504, LFNM 260–61, CLC 70, A&G §546). Render *cum* into English here
    as *when*. **rēgnāsset** – contracted form of the pluperfect subjunctive: the
    -v- ending of a perfect stem is often dropped before *-i-* or *-ā-* (*rēgnāvisset*
    → *rēgnāsset*) (A&G §181). As often, translate the subjunctive in the *cum*
    clause as the corresponding indicative (*had ruled*).

trīgintā et duōs annōs – *accusative of duration of time* (W 314, ER 345, LFA 97, LFNM 495, CLC 149, A&G §423).

29. **fulmine ictus cum domō suā ārsit** – The perfect passive participle (*ictus*) indicates an action that has been completed before that of the main verb (*ārsit*). The participle can be translated as a subordinate clause (*after he had been struck by lightning*), or the entire sentence can be rendered into English as two coordinate clauses (*he was struck by lightning and burned together, etc.*). **fulmine** – *ablative of means or instrument* (W 116–17, ER 346, LFA 20, LFNM 486, CLC 326–27, A&G §409). **ictus** – perfect passive participle of *īcō, -ere*. **ārsit** – perfect of *ārdeō, -ēre*.

Chapter V

30. **Ancus Mārcius** – Like that of his predecessor, Ancus Marcius's name comes from a plebeian gens that rose to prominence long after the reign of the seven kings would have been established in the tradition. His name, therefore, is also probably that of a real person and not a later interpolation.

suscēpit – perfect active of *suscipiō, -ere.*

31. **Contrā Latīnōs dīmicāvit** – The Latins were the inhabitants of the plain of Latium (modern-day Lazio), who shared a common language and common religious practices. Their numerous villages and cities formed confederations, which later historians came to know as the Latin League. The leadership of the league had passed early on from Alba to Rome (see chapter IV). During the later Regal period and the early Republic, Rome and the Latin League variously established treaty relationships and engaged in conflicts. This culminated with the defeat and abolition of the league by Rome in 338 BCE. For more information, see the entry for *Latini* in the *Oxford Classical Dictionary*, 3rd Edition (New York: Oxford University Press, 1996).

Aventīnum montem cīvitātī adiēcit et Iāniculum – *Aventīnum montem*
and *Iāniculum* are the direct objects of *adiēcit*, *cīvitātī* the *dative of
indirect object*. **adiēcit** – perfect active of *adiciō, -ere*. For the locations of
the hills of Rome, see Appendix A: Maps.

---

32. **apud ōstium Tiberis cīvitātem . . . condidit** – According to tradition, Ostia, Rome's principal port city, was founded during the
reign of Ancus Marcius (642–616 BCE). There is no archeological
evidence of settlements there, however, until well into the Republic.
See Appendix A: Maps.

---

cīvitātem – direct object of *condidit*. For *cīvitās* as a synonym of *urbs*, see
note on *cīvitāte*, line 7.

Chapter VI

---

34. **Deinde rēgnum Prīscus Tarquinius accēpit** – According to tradition, Tarquinius Priscus was the first Etruscan king of Rome. The
Etruscans were Rome's powerful neighbors to the north who inhabited the area roughly equivalent to modern-day Tuscany. Since
Rome was one of the northernmost Latin cities (see Appendix A:
Maps), Etruria exerted a more powerful influence on it than on
many of the other Latin cities. The historian H. H. Scullard writes
that "the Romans borrowed much, but they remained essentially
Latin, in race, language, institutions, and religion. But their relations with the Latins were gradually altered, for the Etruscans had
reorientated the city. Previously it had been a northern outpost of
the Latins against Etruria; it became a southern outpost of Etruria
against the Latins. The spear-head was turned from north to south"

---

continued

(*A History of the Roman World: 753 to 146 BC*, pp. 54–55). For more information, see the entry for *Etruscans* in the *Oxford Classical Dictionary*, 3rd Edition (New York: Oxford University Press, 1996).

numerum senātōrum duplicāvit – There is no consensus among the Roman historians about how or when the senate was increased from its original one hundred members. Most agree that Tarquinius Priscus increased the number of senators by one hundred (by admitting the *gentes minores*—families that, for an unknown reason, were less prominent than those from the original senatorial families, the *gentes maiores*). By all accounts the number of senators had reached three hundred by the early Republic.

35. **circum Rōmae aedificāvit** – A circus was an enclosure for chariot racing. The oldest circus at Rome was the Circus Maximus, between the Palatine and Aventine Hills. Tradition assigns its construction to Tarquinus Priscus. By republican times the Circus Maximus was the largest structure at Rome, accommodating approximately 150,000 spectators.

lūdōs Rōmānōs – The Lūdī Rōmānī were among the oldest and most important games celebrated at Rome. Dedicated to Jupiter Optimus Maximus, they were a combination of religious festivals, chariot racing, and public parades. According to tradition, they were introduced during the reign of Tarquinius Priscus. While they do seem to be of Etruscan origin, their regular observance probably dates to the Republic.

35. **Rōmae** – *locative* (W 314, ER 349, LFA 178, LFNM 26–28, CLC 327, A&G §427): *at Rome.*

36. **Vīcit īdem etiam Sabīnōs** – The Sabine villages were mainly north-east of Rome, along the Apennine Mountains. See Appendix A: Maps.

īdem – *Īdem, eadem, idem* is often used to introduce further information about a subject or object; translate as *furthermore, also, at the same time* (see also *nōbilissimam fēminam Lucrētiam eandemque pudīcissimam*, line 52).

nōn parum agrōrum sublātum īsdem urbis Rōmae territōriō iūnxit – *Nōn parum agrōrum* is the object of *iūnxit* and is modified by the participle *sublātum*. This participle can be rendered into English as a relative clause (*which had been taken*), or the entire sentence can be translated into coordinate clauses (*he took a large amount of land, etc., and added it . . .*). Compare to *fulmine ictus cum domō suā ārsit*, line 29. The English word order would be *iūnxit territōriō urbis Rōmae nōn parum agrōrum sublātum īsdem*. **nōn parum** – *not a small amount* = *large amount*. The expression of an idea by negating its opposite is called *litotes*. **agrōrum** – *partitive genitive* (W 124, ER 342, LFA 25, CLC 324, A&G §346). **īsdem** – alternate form of *eīsdem;* the construction is *ablative of separation* with the participle *sublātum* (W 163, ER 348, LFA 214, CLC 326–27, A&G §400): *taken from the same people*. **urbis Rōmae** – genitives modifying *territōriō*. **territōriō** – *dative of indirect object* with *iūnxit: added to the territory.*

37. **triumphāns urbem intrāvit** – A successful Roman general would make a triumphal procession—which in republican times proceeded along the Via Sacra to the temple of Jupiter Capitolinus—upon his return from a campaign. The ceremony had Etruscan origins, as the tradition suggests.

38. **Mūrōs fēcit et cloācās, Capitōlium inchoāvit** – The Capitoline was the hill on which Tarquinius Priscus was said to have begun the great temple to Jupiter Optimus Maximus. The building of the *cloacae*—to

continued

> drain the valley between the Palatine and Capitoline Hills—was, in fact, a prerequisite for the construction projects on the Capitoline.

39. **per Ancī filiōs** – The *personal agent* is often expressed by *per* with the accusative (LFA 33, A&G §405b).

    occīsus est – perfect passive of *occīdō, -ere.*

    rēgis eius – in apposition to *Ancī* (W 19, LFA 8, A&G §282).

    cuī – *dative with a compound verb* (W 296, ER 343, LFA 173, CLC 325, A&G §370). Translate as if it were the direct object of *successerat.*

Chapter VII

> 41. **Post hunc Servius Tullius suscēpit imperium** – The name of the sixth king of Rome is Latin, not Etruscan, perhaps signaling an interruption in Etruscan rule. Servius is also credited with building a temple to Diana—a Latin, rather than Etruscan, goddess—on the Aventine. The historicity of Servius Tullius, considered certain by most historians, is again supported by his plebeian name.

> **genitus ex nōbilī fēminā, captīvā tamen et ancillā** – According to tradition, Servius's mother was a Latin noblewoman taken captive in war and given to the wife of Tarquinius Priscus.

    genitus – perfect passive participle of *gīgnō, -ere.*

42. **captīvā . . . et ancillā** – modifies *fēminā.*

    subēgit – perfect of *subagō, -ere.*

> **montēs trēs, Quirīnālem, Vīminālem, Ēsquilīnum, urbī adiūnxit** – Servius is said to have expanded the pomerium, the sacred boundary of the city, to include the Quirinal, Viminal, and (part of) the Esquiline hills. This does not correspond to the so-called Servian Walls,

> which were actually constructed in the fourth century BCE. See Appendix A: Maps.

43. **Quirīnālem, Vīminālem, Ēsquilīnum** – in apposition to *montēs trēs* (W 25, LFA 8, A&G §282).

urbī – *dative of indirect object.*

> **fossās circum mūrum dūxit** – Eutropius's description of Servius having made *fossae* (ditches) around the city is probably more historical than the stone walls traditionally attributed to this king. The fossae would also have consisted of *aggerēs* (protective earthen ramparts).

> **44. Prīmus omnium cēnsum ōrdināvit** – According to tradition, Servius carried out the census in order to classify the citizen body within the new political assembly, the Comitia Centuriata. While many modern scholars accept that Servius implemented some version of constitutional reform whereby the citizen body was divided by capacity to arm oneself, the complex system of graded property classes on which the later Comitia Centuriata was based probably does not belong to the Regal period. For more information, see the entry for *Comitia* in the *Oxford Classical Dictionary*, 3rd Edition (New York: Oxford University Press, 1996).

> **quī adhūc per orbem terrārum incognitus erat** – There were censuses in the Greek world that predated the reign of Servius Tullius. Perhaps Eutropius is pointing out that Servius's reforms were supposed to have taken place before the reforms of Cleisthenes at Athens.

45. **incognitus erat** – This is an adjective with the imperfect of *sum, esse,* not a pluperfect passive verbal form.

Rōma . . . habuit capita LXXXIII mīlia – *Rōma* is the subject and *capita LXXXIII* the direct object of *habuit.*

omnibus in cēnsum dēlātīs – *ablative absolute* (W 193–94, ER 348, LFA 33, LFNM 298–99, CLC 218, A&G §419). **dēlātīs** – perfect passive participle of *dēferō, -ferre.*

---

46. **capita LXXXIII mīlia cīvium Rōmānōrum** – This number would include all male citizens; it is close to those given by both Livy and Dionysius of Halicarnassus. The number may, however, be too high for the Regal period.

---

cīvium Rōmānōrum – genitive modifying *capita.*

47. **Occīsus est** – perfect passive of *occīdō, -ere.*

scelere – *ablative of means or instrument* (W 116–17, ER 346, LFA 20, LFNM 486, CLC 326–27, A&G §409).

generī suī Tarquiniī Superbī – genitives modifying *scelere.*

filiī eius rēgis – in apposition to *generī* (W 25, LFA 8, A&G §282).

cuī – *dative with a compound verb* (W 296, ER 343, LFA 173, CLC 325, A&G §370). Translate as if it were the direct object of *successerat.*

Occīsus est scelere generī suī Tarquiniī Superbī – Beginning with his treacherous accession to power, Tarquinius Superbus is portrayed as a Greek tyrant. The Greek historian Polybius, writing about the Roman constitution, drew an explicit comparison between Tarquinius Superbus and the tyrants of the Archaic Greek city-states: "Such is the cycle of political revolution, the course appointed by nature in which constitutions change. . . . The kingship changed into a tyranny; the first steps towards its overthrow were taken by the subjects, and conspiracies began to be formed" (*Histories* VI.7, translated by W. R. Paton).

Chapter VIII

49. **L. Tarquinius Superbus, septimus atque ultimus rēgum** – The narrative of the two Tarquins contains a good deal of duplication: they are said to have undertaken some of the same building projects, conquered some of the same peoples, and so forth. The historian R. M. Ogilvie says, "Their very names, Priscus [ancient] and Superbus [proud], are the work of subsequent differentiation. . . . We should rather believe that tradition accurately preserved the memory of an Etruscan era at Rome lasting for a century with possible interruptions (Servius Tullius) during which the Tarquin family maintained a dynastic rule, but that the few specific events which were remembered, such as . . . the tragedy of Lucretia, were remembered as occurring in the times of the Tarquins rather than as attached to one particular person" (*Commentary on Livy, Books 1–5* [New York: Oxford University Press, 1965], p. 145).

L. – Roman praenomina were almost always written in abbreviated form, except when they appeared alone. Lucius is one of several Roman praenomina of Etruscan origin.

Volscōs, quae gēns ad Campāniam euntibus nōn longē ab urbe est, vīcit – The Volsci were a people who inhabited southern Latium. During the early Republic, they were to become one of Rome's principal threats in Latium. See Appendix A: Maps.

Volscōs – object of *vīcit*.

50. **ad Campāniam euntibus** – *Euntibus* is the dative of the present participle of *eō, īre. Ad . . . euntibus* and *ab . . . venientibus* are often used to show relative location: *as one goes to* and *as one comes from* (A&G §378.2).

Gabiōs – in apposition to *cīvitātem*.

> **51. cum Tuscīs pācem fēcit** – The fact that Rome may have been at
> war with Etruscan cities (such as Veii) is not contradicted by Etruscan
> rule at Rome. Etruscan cities were often at war with one another.

52. **Posteā, Ardeam oppugnāns . . . imperium perdidit** – The English word
    order would be *Posteā, oppugnāns Ardeam, cīvitātem positam in octāvō
    decimō mīliāriō ab urbe Rōmā, perdidit imperium.*

54. **cum . . . stuprāsset** – *cum clause (circumstantial)* (W 255–56, ER 361,
    LFA 504, LFNM 260–61, CLC 70, A&G §546). **stuprāsset** – contracted
    form of the pluperfect subjunctive (A&G §181). See note on *rēgnāsset*,
    line 29.

> **Tarquinius iūnior** – According to most Roman historical accounts,
> Sextus Tarquinius was the youngest son of Tarquinius Superbus.

> **nōbilissimam fēminam Lucrētiam** – The story of the rape of Lucre-
> tia is deeply established in the Roman tradition, and it is assumed
> that Lucretia was a historical person (though it is impossible to de-
> termine what role she may have actually played in the downfall of
> the monarchy). The story has many antecedents in Greek literature,
> and it is one of the key episodes that characterize the reign of Tar-
> quinius Superbus as a tyrannical one.

55. **eandemque** – *Īdem, eadem, idem* is often used to introduce further
    information about a subject or object; translate as *furthermore, also, at
    the same time* (see also *Vīcit īdem etiam Sabīnōs*, line 36).

> **Collātīnī** – The historicity of Lucius Tarquinius Collatinus, the hus-
> band of Lucretia and one of the first two consuls, is dubious.

56. **marītō et patrī et amīcīs** – *datives of indirect object.*

questa fuisset – pluperfect subjunctive of the deponent verb *queror, querī;* the auxiliaries *fuissem, fuissēs,* etc., are sometimes used for *essem, essēs,* etc., in the formation of the pluperfect passive (A&G §184, note).

57. **Propter quam causam** – The relative *quī, quae, quod* often stands at the beginning of a sentence, serving to connect it with the preceding one (LFA 204, CLC 309, A&G §308f). Translate into English as *this: [and] on account of this reason.*

> **Brūtus, parēns et ipse Tarquiniī** – According to tradition, Lucius Junius Brutus was the grandson of Tarquinius Priscus. Both his gens and his family name, however, are Latin, not Etruscan. The tradition that he feigned madness to escape persecution by the king arose to explain his family name, Brutus (which means *stupid*). There is little doubt that Brutus was a historical person or that he was involved in the establishment of the Republic. His descendant was Marcus Junius Brutus the tyrannicide, one of the principal leaders of the conspiracy against Julius Caesar in 44 BCE.

parēns – *Parēns* meaning *relative* is a late usage (in classical Latin, *parēns* means *parent*). Notice that the word for *relative* in many Romance languages come from this late usage: *parente, pariente, parent.*

58. **Tarquiniō** – *dative of separation* (W 291, ER 343, CLC 325, A&G §381). Some compound verbs meaning *to take away* govern the dative of separation.

eum – The antecedent is *Tarquinius.*

59. **quī** – The antecedent is *exercitus.*

60. **portīs clausīs** – *ablative absolute* (W 193–94, ER 348, LFA 33, LFNM 298–99, CLC 218, A&G §419).

exclūsus est – perfect passive of *exclūdō, -ere.*

cumque imperāsset – *cum clause (circumstantial)* (W 255–56, ER 361, LFA 504, LFNM 260–61, CLC 70, A&G §546). **imperāsset** – contracted form of the pluperfect subjunctive (A&G §181). See note on *rēgnāsset,* line 29.

annōs quattuor et vīgintī – *accusative of duration of time* (W 314, ER 345, LFA 97, LFNM 495, CLC 149, A&G §423).

61. **līberīs** – This is the noun *līberī, -ōrum, children,* not the adjective *līber, -era, -um, free.*

rēgnātum est – perfect passive of *rēgnō, -āre.* The passive forms of intransitive verbs are often used impersonally (LFNM 503, A&G §208d).

per septem rēgēs – The *personal agent* is often expressed by *per* with the accusative (LFA 33, A&G §405b).

62. **annīs ducentīs quadrāgintā tribus** – Occasionally, the ablative is used to express duration of time (A&G §424b).

cum . . . possidēret – *cum clause (circumstantial)* (W 255–56, ER 361, LFA 504, LFNM 260–61, CLC 73, A&G §546). **possidēret** – imperfect subjunctive of *possideō, -ēre.*

Chapter IX

64. **Hinc cōnsulēs coepēre, prō ūnō rēge duo** – According to the Roman tradition, the monarchy was immediately replaced by dual supreme magistrates (probably originally called *praetors,* not *consuls*). This is accepted by many, though not all, modern historians. The consuls were the highest civil authority of the Republic and also the supreme commanders of the army. They gave their names to the years in which they served (e.g., *C. Fabiō et L. Virgīniō cōnsulibus, in the consulships of Gaius Fabius and Lucius Virginius*). For more information, see the entry for *Consul* in the *Oxford Classical Dictionary,* 3rd Edition (New York: Oxford University Press, 1996).

coepēre – The ending *-ēre* is often used instead of *-ērunt* for the third-person plural perfect active indicative. *Coepī, -isse* is a defective verb with only perfect tenses (*incipiō* fills in for the present, imperfect, and future tenses) (A&G §205).

ut . . . alter eum . . . coercēret – *purpose clause* (W 229–30, ER 362, LFA 77, LFNM 40–41, CLC 110, A&G §531.1).

sī ūnus malus esse voluisset – The pluperfect subjunctive is used in this if clause because the clause is in a subordinate construction (a purpose clause after *ut*). It is used to show that an action has been completed before the time of the then clause. Had the condition not been in a subordinate construction, the if clause here would have been either future perfect indicative or perfect subjunctive (A&G §516 2c).

66. **placuit** – *Placeō, -ēre* is often used impersonally (especially in historic tenses) to indicate resolutions of the senate. It may be followed by an infinitive or by *ut* or *nē* plus the subjunctive (as here). The same meaning is used at line 71.

nē imperium . . . habērent and **sed cīvīlēs semper essent** – *jussive noun clauses (indirect command)* (W 253, ER 364, LFA 135, LFNM 98, CLC 221, A&G §563).

nē . . . īnsolentiōrēs redderentur – *purpose clause* (W 229–30, ER 362, LFA 77, LFNM 40–41, CLC 221, A&G §531.1). **īnsolentiōrēs** – predicate nominative (W 34, ER 341, LFNM 473, CLC 324, A&G §283).

67. **quī sē . . . scīrent** – *relative clause of characteristic* (W 323–24, LFA 504, LFNM 508, A&G §535).

68. **sē . . . futūrōs esse** – *indirect statement* (W 202–4, ER 366, LFA 117, A&G §577–84) after *scīrent; sē* is the accusative subject; *futūrōs esse* is the future infinitive of *sum, esse*: render into English as either *that they were going to be* or *that they would be*.

prīvātōs – predicate accusative (A&G §392) with *sē*.

Fuērunt igitur, annō prīmō . . . marītus Lucrētiae – The English word order would be *Annō prīmō igitur expulsīs rēgibus cōnsulēs fuērunt L. Iūnius Brūtus, quī maximē ēgerat ut Tarquinius pellerētur, et Tarquinius Collātīnus, marītus Lucrētiae.*

annō prīmō – *ablative of time when* (no preposition is used) (W 125, ER 346, LFA 7, LFNM 496, CLC 326–27, A&G §423).

69. **expulsīs rēgibus** – *ablative absolute* (W 193–94, ER 348, LFA 33, LFNM 298–99, CLC 218, A&G §419).

    ēgerat – pluperfect indicative of *agō, -ere*.

    ut Tarquinius pellerētur – *purpose clause* (W 229–30, ER 362, LFA 77, LFNM 40–41, CLC 110, A&G §531.1). The imperfect subjunctive may be rendered here with the English auxiliary *might: that Tarquinius might be expelled.* More natural English would use the active voice and an infinitive: *to expel Tarquinius.*

70. **Tarquiniō** – *dative of separation* (W 291, ER 343, CLC 325, A&G §381). Some compound verbs meaning *to take away* govern the dative of separation.

71. **sublāta est** – perfect passive of *sufferō, -ferre; dignitās* is the subject.

    dignitās – Like *honor, dignitās* is often used to mean *a position conferring rank* or *a high political office.*

    nē quisquam in urbe remanēret – *jussive noun clauses (indirect command)* (W 303–4, ER 364, LFA 135, LFNM 98, CLC 221, A&G §563): *that no one should remain in the city. Nē quisquam* is a more emphatic expression of *nē quis.*

72. **quī Tarquinius vocārētur** – *relative clause of characteristic* (W 323–24, LFA 504, LFNM 508, A&G §535). Translate here with an English indicative, *who were called,* rather than using the auxiliary *would.*

    acceptō omnī patrimōniō suō – *ablative absolute* (W 193–94, ER 348, LFA 33, LFNM 298–99, CLC 218, A&G §419). **acceptō** – perfect passive participle of *accipiō, -ere.*

---

73. **locō ipsīus factus est L. Valerius Pūblicola cōnsul** – Livy gives the praenomen of Valerius Publicola as Publius, not Lucius. He also mentions a popular etymology that derives the family name Pūblicola from *populus + colō (favorer* or *friend of the people)* because of Valerius Publicola's efforts on behalf of the plebeian citizen body. These efforts included the enactment of the Valerian Law, which granted the right of appeal to all citizens. For the division of the Roman citizen body into two classes, patrician and plebeian, see chapter XIII.

factus est – perfect passive of *faciō, -ere; Valerius Pūblicola* is the subject, *cōnsul* the predicate nominative (W 34, ER 341, LFNM 473, CLC 324, A&G §283).

74. **urbī Rōmae** – *dative with a compound verb* (W 296, ER 343, LFA 173, CLC 325, A&G §370).

rēx Tarquinius – here, Tarquinius Superbus.

fuerat expulsus – pluperfect passive indicative of *expellō, -ere;* the auxiliaries *fuissem, fuissēs,* etc., are sometimes used for *essem, essēs,* etc., in the formation of the pluperfect passive (A&G §184, note).

75. **ut in rēgnum posset restituī** – *purpose clause* (W 229–30, ER 362, LFA 77, LFNM 40–41, CLC 110, A&G §531.1). Translate either with the English auxiliary *might* (*in order that he might be able to be restored*) or with an English infinitive (*to be able to be restored*). **restituī** – present passive infinitive of *restituō, -ere.*

Chapter X

77. **Brūtum mātrōnae Rōmānae . . . lūxērunt** – The English word order would be *Rōmānae mātrōnae lūxērunt Brūtum (dēfēnsōrem suae pudīcitiae) per annum, quasi commūnem patrem.*

78. **dēfēnsōrem** – in apposition to *Brūtum.*

79. **lūxērunt** – perfect of *lūgeō, -ēre.*

> **Sp. Lucrētium Tricipitīnum** – Like Lucretia's husband Collatinus, her father Spurius Lucretius Tricipitinus is of doubtful historicity.

80. **quō . . . mortuō** – *ablative absolute* (W 193–94, ER 348, LFA 33, LFNM 298–99, CLC 218, A&G §419): *and with this man having died.* The relative *quī, quae, quod* often stands at the beginning of a sentence or clause, serving to connect it with the preceding one (LFA 204, CLC 218, A&G §308f).

morbō – *ablative of cause* (W 493, ER 346, LFA 499, LFNM 495, A&G §404): *by natural causes.*

> **Horātium Pulvillum** – Marcus Horatius Pulvillus is credited with dedicating the temple to Jupiter Optimus Maximus, which had been built during the reign of the Tarquins (see chapters VI and VIII). His historicity is likely.

81. **collēgam** – *predicate accusative* (ER 366, A&G §392–93).

> **prīmus annus quīnque cōnsulēs habuit** – The tradition that the first year of the Republic had five consuls probably arose to accommodate the several figures—some historical, some later inventions—that had come to be associated with the establishment of the Republic.

prīmus annus quīnque cōnsulēs habuit – *Prīmus annus* is the subject of *habuit; quīnque cōnsulēs* is the direct object.

82. **cum . . . cessisset . . . perīsset . . . mortuus esset** – *cum clauses (causal)* (W 255–56, ER 361, LFA 504, LFNM 265, A&G §549). Render *cum* here as *since.*

urbe – *ablative of separation* (W 163, ER 348, LFA 214, CLC 326–27, A&G §400).

83. **perīsset** – contracted pluperfect form of *periisset; -ii* before *-s* is regularly contracted to *-ī* (A&G §203).

mortuus esset – pluperfect subjunctive of the deponent verb *morior, morī.*

Chapter XI

84. **Secundō quoque annō . . . Rōmam paene cēpit** – The English word order would be *Secundō annō quoque Tarquinius iterum intulit bellum Rōmānīs ut reciperētur in rēgnum, Porsennā rēge Tusciae ferente auxilium eī, et paene cēpit Rōmam.*

Secundō . . . annō – *ablative of time when* (no preposition is used) (W 125, ER 346, LFA 7, LFNM 496, CLC 326–27, A&G §423).

ut reciperētur in rēgnum – *purpose clause* (W 229–30, ER 362, LFA 77, LFNM 40–41, CLC 110, A&G §531.1).

85. **bellum Rōmānīs intulit** – *Bellum* is the object of *intulit, Rōmānīs* the *dative of indirect object.*

auxilium eī ferente Porsennā – *ablative absolute* (W 193–94, ER 348, LFA 33, LFNM 298–99, CLC 218, A&G §419). **ferente** – present active participle of *ferō, ferre.* Notice that the active form of the participle can be used to form an *ablative absolute;* here *auxilium* is the object of the participle: *with Porsenna offering him help.*

rēge – in apposition to *Porsennā.*

Porsennā – Lars Porsenna, the king of the Etruscan city Clusium, besieged Rome during the very early Republic. Eutropius follows the main Roman tradition, in which Porsenna called off the siege, an attempt to reinstate Tarquinius Superbus, after witnessing the bravery of Roman citizens like Gaius Mucius (see the boxed text *Romanus sum civis,* page 18). More likely is the alternate tradition in which Porsenna captured Rome and imposed harsh peace terms. The fact that he did not then reinstate Tarquinius suggests that Porsenna was not fighting on his behalf.

---

86. **victus est** – perfect passive of *vincō, -ere.*

Tertiō annō post rēgēs exāctōs – Through chapter XV of Book I, Eutropius uses the expression *since the expulsion of the kings* to give the date. In chapter XVIII he switches to the more widely used formulation *from the founding of the city.* **Tertiō annō** – *ablative of time when* (no preposition is used) (W 125, ER 346, LFA 7, LFNM 496, CLC 326–27, A&G §423). **exāctōs** – perfect passive participle of *exigō, -ere.*

87. **cum suscipī nōn posset . . . neque eī Porsenna . . . praestāret auxilium** – *cum clauses (causal)* (W 255–56, ER 361, LFA 504, LFNM 265, A&G §549). Render *cum* here as *since.* **suscipī** – present passive infinitive of *suscipiō, -ere.*

88. **fēcerat** – pluperfect of *faciō, -ere.*

Tusculum – Tusculum was an important city in Latium, approximately fifteen miles southeast of Rome. Its tyrant, Tarquinius Superbus's father-in-law, was said to have supported Tarquinius in his attempt to regain the throne.

Tusculum sē contulit, quae cīvitās nōn longē ab urbe est – The noun *cīvitās*, which describes *Tusculum*, logically belongs outside the relative clause: *Tusculum sē contulit, cīvitātem quae nōn longē ab urbe est.* However, the antecedent of a relative pronoun—especially an appositive—is often incorporated into the relative clause (A&G §307e).

Tusculum – *accusative of place to which:* no preposition is used with the names of cities (W 314, ER 345, LFA 204, LFNM 478, CLC 325, A&G §427).

90. **cōnsenuit** – perfect of *cōnsenescō, -ere.*

91. **cum Sabīnī Rōmānīs bellum intulissent** – *cum clause (circumstantial)* (W 255–56, ER 361, LFA 504, LFNM 260–61, CLC 70, A&G §546). *Sabīnī* is the subject and *bellum* the direct object of *intulissent; Rōmānīs* is the *dative of indirect object.* **intulissent** – perfect of *īnferō, -ferre.*

Sabīnī . . . victī sunt et dē hīs triumphātum – This victory is recorded in the *Fasti Triumphales* (Records of triumphs). The Sabines, who had not been in conflict with Rome for some time, may have been taking advantage of its weakened position due to its recent conflict with Porsenna.

---

92. **victī sunt** – perfect passive of *vincō, -ere.*

triumphātum est – perfect passive of *triumphō, -āre.* The passive forms of intransitive verbs are often used impersonally (LFNM 503, A&G §208d).

L. Valerius ille – *Ille* following a noun often means *the famous* (A&G §297b).

93. **collēga** – in apposition to *L. Valerius.*

mortuus est – perfect of the deponent verb *morior, morī.*

ut . . . sūmptum habuerit sepultūrae – *result clause* (W 237–38, ER 362, LFA 92, LFNM 319–20, CLC 130, A&G §537.1). A result clause can often be identified by the presence of an adverb indicating degree, such as *adeō,* in the main clause: "He did something to such an extent that he . . ." An imperfect subjunctive (e.g., *habēret*) is normally used to denote action at the same time as that of the historical main verb; the perfect subjunctive (*habuerit*) is used here to emphasize that it is a simple past-tense action (A&G §485c).

---

collātīs ā populō nummīs – The people paid for the burial of Valerius Publicola because he had been their champion. See note on *locō ipsīus factus est L. Valerius Pūblicola cōnsul,* line 73.

---

94. **Quem** – The relative *quī, quae, quod* often stands at the beginning of a sentence or clause, serving to connect it with the preceding one (LFA 204, CLC 309, A&G §308f). Translate into English here as *and him.*

Chapter XII

96. **cum gener Tarquiniī . . . ingentem collēgisset exercitum** – *cum clause (circumstantial)* (W 255–56, ER 361, LFA 504, LFNM 260–61, CLC 70, A&G §546). **collēgisset** – pluperfect subjunctive of *colligō, -ere.*

ad iniūriam socerī vindicandam – The gerundive with *ad* or *causā* is often used to express *purpose* (W 334, LFA 142, A&G §506). It is best to take the entire gerundive phrase into account and render it into idiomatic English: *for avenging the wrong done to his father-in-law* (using an English gerund) or *to avenge the wrong done to his father-in-law* (using an English infinitive). An overly literal translation of the gerundive would be *for [the purpose of] the wrong done to his father-in-law to be avenged.*

socerī – *objective genitive* (W 492, A&G §347–48).

97. **Rōmae** – *locative* (W 314, ER 349, LFA 178, LFNM 26–28, CLC 327, A&G §427): *at Rome.*

---

98. **quae dictātūra appellātur, maior quam cōnsulātus** – The dictatorship was an extraordinary political office employed during military or political crises. The dictator held undivided military authority—not subject to veto or appeal—for six months. The title may have originally been *magister populi*. The origins of this office are obscure, though as the tradition suggests, it does seem to be a republican institution, not a temporary reversion to monarchy, since the office existed in other Latin cities.

Eōdem annō etiam magister equitum factus est – The *magister equitum* was the dictator's second-in-command. He was nominated by the dictator upon the latter's appointment to office. As the title suggests, the *magister equitum* may have originally been in command of the cavalry.

---

99. **equitum** – genitive plural of *eques, equitis.*

    quī dictātōrī obsequerētur – *purpose clause* introduced by the relative pronoun (W 328, LFNM 509, CLC 179, A&G §531.2). Like *ut-purpose clauses,* this may be rendered into English with the infinitive: *to be subordinate to the dictator.* **dictātōrī** – dative with the compound verb *obsequerētur* (W 296, ER 343, LFA 173, LFNM 509, CLC 325, A&G §370).

100. **Rōmae** – *locative* (W 314, ER 349, LFA 178, LFNM 26–28, CLC 327, A&G §427): *at Rome* (also in line 101).

Chapter XIII

101. **sēditiōnem populus Rōmae fēcit** – The Roman citizen body was divided into two classes: plebeians and patricians. The political history of the early Republic was dominated by the so-called conflict of the orders, in which the plebeians attempted to strengthen their political, social, and economic position. According to tradition, in 494 BCE the plebeians seceded to a hill near Rome, the Mons Sacra, and formed a virtual state within a state.

102. **fēcit** – perfect of *faciō, -ere*.

> **tamquam . . . premerētur** – *Tamquam* regularly governs the subjunctive, meaning *as if* (A&G §540.2). As here, it sometimes introduces a circumstance alleged to be the ground on which an act is based; translate as *on the grounds that*. See *tamquam* in the *Oxford Latin Dictionary* (New York: Oxford University Press, 1982).

> **ipse** – the antecedent is *populus*.

ipse sibi tribūnōs plēbis quasi propriōs iūdicēs et dēfēnsōrēs creāvit – During their secession, the plebeians established their own assemblies and officers. In the agreement by which they returned, the senate recognized the newly created tribunes as the representatives of the plebeian order. The tribunes exercised veto power over laws, elections, and acts of magistrates, elicited resolutions (*plebiscita*), and summoned the plebs to assembly (*comitia plebis tributa*). For more information, see the entry for *Plebs* in the *Oxford Classical Dictionary*, 3rd Edition (New York: Oxford University Press, 1996).

103. **per quōs . . . tūtus esse posset** – *purpose clause* introduced by the relative pronoun (W 328, LFNM 509, CLC 179, A&G §531.2): *through whom they might be able to be safe*.

Chapter XIV

105. **Sequentī** – present active participle of *sequor, sequī.*

> **Volscī contrā Rōmānōs bellum reparāvērunt** – The Volsci were one of Rome's principal threats in the region. The tradition that the Romans and the Volsci had been in conflict since the late Regal period is probably correct (see chapter VIII). The Roman general Coriolanus is credited with having captured the Volscian city Corioli.

106. **Coriolōs** – The names of some cities are plural, such as *Bāiae, Coriolī, Fīdēnae, Pompēiī,* and *Veiī.*

Chapter XV

107. **ēiectī erant** – pluperfect passive indicative of *ēiciō, -ere.*

   expulsus ex urbe . . . auxilia contrā Rōmānōs accēpit – The English word order would be *Q. Mārcius—dux Rōmānus quī cēperat Coriolōs, cīvitātem Volscōrum—expulsus ex urbe, īrātus contendit ad Volscōs ipsōs et accēpit auxilia contrā Rōmānōs.* **expulsus** – perfect passive participle of *expellō, -ere.*

> 108. **Q. Mārcius** – Livy gives Marcius Coriolanus's praenomen as Gnaeus, not Quintus. According to the Roman tradition, he received the agnomen Coriolanus after his victory over the Volsci at Corioli (see chapter XIV). In the original myth, however, Coriolanus may have been a Volscian—the eponymous founder of Corioli, not its captor. He was said to have been expelled from Rome later for opposing grain distribution to the starving plebeians. Shakespeare made him the protagonist of the play *The Tragedy of Coriolanus.*

109. **accēpit** – perfect of *accipiō, -ere;* the subject is *Q. Mārcius,* the object *auxilia.*

110. **vīcit** – perfect of *vincō, -ere.*

    accessit – perfect of *accēdō, -ere.*

    oppugnātūrus etiam patriam suam – A future participle may sometimes stand for the then clause (apodosis) of a condition (A&G §498.3): *ready to attack . . . if his mother had not come.* The usual formation of this past *contrary-to-fact condition* would have been *oppugnāvisset . . . nisi māter Veturia vēnissent: he would have attacked . . . if his mother Veturia had not come* (A&G §517).

111. **lēgātīs . . . repudiātīs** – *ablative absolute* (W 193–94, ER 348, LFA 33, LFNM 298–99, CLC 218, A&G §419).

---

113. **remōvit exercitum** – According to Livy, the Volsci executed Coriolanus for calling off the siege.

---

114. **quī dux . . . esset** – *relative clause of characteristic* (W 323, LFA 504, LFNM 508, A&G §535): *who would be a military commander.*

Chapter XVI

115. **C. Fabiō [Vibulanō] et L. Virgīniō [Tricostō Rutilō] cōnsulibus** – Livy gives the praenomina of these two consuls as Caeso and Titus, respectively. Identifying the consuls for a specific year is one of the regular methods for giving the date. The construction is *ablative absolute.* Since classical Latin lacks the present participle of *sum, esse* (cf. the English word *being*), two nouns or a noun and an adjective in the ablative case can function as an *ablative absolute:* for instance, *Tarquiniō rēge, with Tarquinius [being] king* (W 193–94, ER 349, LFA 33, LFNM 298–99, CLC 218, A&G §419a).

---

116. **contrā Vēientēs** – Veii, Rome's nearest Etruscan neighbor, had been struggling with Rome for several years over supremacy in the region around the Tiber. See Appendix A: Maps.

---

sōlī – modifies *trecentī nōbilēs hominēs*.

suscēpērunt – perfect of *suscipiō, -ere*.

117. **senātuī et populō** – *datives of indirect object* with the present participle *prōmittentēs*.

per sē omne certāmen implendum [esse] – *indirect statement* (W 202–4, ER 366, LFA 117, A&G §577–84). The future passive participle *implendum* is indicating action after that of *prōmittentēs: promising that the entire battle would be carried out by themselves*. A more usual formation would employ *sē* as the accusative subject and a future active infinitive: *prōmittentēs sē omne certāmen implētūrōs esse: promising that they would carry out the entire battle*.

profectī – perfect participle of the deponent verb *proficīscor, -ficīscī*.

118. **quī singulī magnōrum exercituum ducēs esse dēbērent** – The imperfect subjunctive is often used to denote an unfulfilled obligation (A&G §439b) or an action that was possible or conceivable in past time (A&G §446).

---

119. **Ūnus omnīnō superfuit ex tantā familiā** – The date of the Cremera disaster—and indeed the tradition itself—may be confirmed by the fact that the name *Fabius*, which appears in the *Fasti* (a list of consuls and important events) frequently until 479 BCE, is missing for the next eleven years. The battle may have been a mission that the Fabii volunteered for, which was aimed at raiding and seizing an enemy stronghold. The number *306*—and other details—perhaps developed to connect and synchronize the event with the Battle of Thermopylae in Greece, which occurred at nearly the same time.

---

120. **dūcī** – present passive infinitive of *dūcō, -ere*.

potuerat – pluperfect of *possum, posse*.

121. **habitus est** – perfect passive of *habeō, -ēre*.

---

inventa sunt cīvium capita CXVII mīlia CCCXIX – This is the number that Livy gives for the census of 459 BCE. It may be meant to include women and children.

---

inventa sunt – perfect passive of *inveniō, -īre;* the subject is *cīvium capita CXVII mīlia CCCXIX.*

Chapter XVII

---

122. **Sequentī annō** – Eutropius means the year following the census mentioned in the previous paragraph, that is 558 BCE.

---

cum . . . Rōmānus obsidērētur exercitus – *cum clause (circumstantial)* (W 255–56, ER 361, LFA 504, LFNM 260–61, CLC 73, A&G §546).

---

123. **obsidērētur** – The Roman consul Lucius Minucius was trapped in the valley below Mount Algidus when the Aequi seized the narrow pass at the ridge of the mountain. The Aequi were an Italic people in northeast Latium who were one of Rome's most implacable enemies during the early Republic. See Appendix A: Maps.

L. Quīntius Cincinnātus – The usual spelling of Cincinnatus's gens name is *Quīnctius.* The tradition presents him as the idealized Roman: he reluctantly assumes power, decisively defeats the enemy, and quickly lays aside his office and returns to farming. Nevertheless, the historicity of his person and his defeat of the Aequi are very likely.

---

124. **est factus** – perfect passive of *faciō, -ere*.

quī agrum quattuor iūgerum possidēns manibus suīs colēbat – *Agrum* is the object of both the participle *possidēns* and the verb *colēbat: who, possessing a field of four iugera, used to cultivate [it].* **iūgerum** – *genitive of quality* (A&G §345.b).

manibus suīs – *ablative of means or instrument* (W 116–17, ER 346, LFA 20, LFNM 486, CLC 326–27, A&G §409).

125. **cum in opere et arāns esset inventus** – *cum clause (circumstantial)* (W 255–56, ER 361, LFA 504, LFNM 486, CLC 70, A&G §546). **opere et arāns esset** – A single idea expressed by two nouns and a conjunction (*at work and plowing* = *at work with his plow*) is called *hendiadys.* **esset inventus** – pluperfect passive subjunctive of *inveniō, -īre.*

    sūdōre dētersō – *ablative absolute* (W 193–94, ER 348, LFA 33, LFNM 298–99, CLC 218, A&G §419). **dētersō** – perfect passive participle of *dētergeō, -ēre.*

---

togam praetextam accēpit – The toga praetexta was a purple- or crimson-bordered toga worn by high-ranking magistrates. It was most likely of Etruscan origin.

---

126. **accēpit** – perfect of *accipiō, -ere.*

    caesīs hostibus – *ablative absolute* (W 193–94, ER 348, LFA 33, CLC 218, LFNM 298–99, A&G §419). **caesīs** – perfect passive participle of *caedō, -ere.*

Chapter XVIII

---

127. **ab urbe conditā** – Giving the number of years since the founding of the city is another standard method for establishing the date. Notice the variety with which Eutropius gives the date in the last four paragraphs.

---

conditā – perfect passive participle of *condō, -ere.*

imperium cōnsulāre – subject of *cessāvit.*

---

128. **prō duōbus cōnsulibus decem factī sunt, quī summam potestātem habērent, decemvirī nōminātī** – The Commission of Ten was established to publish the previously unwritten Roman legal code, to protect the plebeians from the arbitrary exercise of power. The regular magistracies were suspended so that the commission could carry out its work without appeal. The decemvirate lasted for two years—according to tradition, there was a good commission in power for the first year and a tyrannical one in power for the second. After a second secession by the plebeians, the decemviri abdicated.

---

factī sunt – perfect passive of *faciō, -ere;* the subject is *decem[virī].*

quī . . . habērent – *purpose clause* introduced by the relative pronoun (W 328, LFNM 509, CLC 179, A&G §531.2): *to hold.*

129. **cum . . . bene ēgissent** – *cum clause (adversative)* (W 255–56, ER 361, LFA 505, LFNM 266–67, A&G §549): *although.* **ēgissent** – pluperfect subjunctive of *agō, -ere.*

130. **ūnus ex hīs** – Most cardinal numbers are followed by *ex* or *dē* plus the ablative to indicate a specific part of a group (W 125, A&G §346c).

Ap. Claudius . . . fīliam virginem corrumpere voluit – Appius Claudius was the leader of the Commission of Ten. Though a historical person, he is portrayed as a stock tyrant in the Roman tradition—the foil to the idealized leadership of Cincinnatus.

Virgīniī cuiusdam – genitives modifying *fīliam virginem.*

quī – The antecedent is *Virgīniī,* not *Ap. Claudius.*

---

131. **contrā Latīnōs in monte Algidō** – Eutropius is mistaken here. The battle of Mons Algidus was fought against the Aequi, not the

---

continued

> Latins. The Romans, Latins, and Hernici (another people from Latium), in fact, were in a defensive alliance during this period. This so-called Triple Alliance had been fighting the Aequi and Volsci for the preceding thirty years.

mīlitārat – contracted form of the pluperfect indicative *mīlitāverat* (A&G §181). See note on *rēgnāsset*, line 29.

132. **quam pater occīdit** – The relative *quī, quae, quod* often stands at the beginning of a sentence or clause, serving to connect it with the preceding one (LFA 204, CLC 309, A&G §308f).

133. **regressus** – perfect participle of the deponent verb *regredior, -gredī*.

Sublāta est – perfect passive of *sufferō, -ferre; potestās* is the subject.

decemvirīs – *dative of separation* (W 291, ER 343, CLC 325, A&G §381). Some compound verbs meaning *to take away* govern the dative of separation.

134. **damnātī sunt** – perfect passive of *damnō, -āre*.

Chapter XIX

135. **ab urbe conditā** – This is the same method of expressing the date as in chapter XVIII. **conditā** – perfect passive participle of *condō, -ere*.

> **Fīdēnātēs contrā Rōmānōs rebellāvērunt** – Fidenae, a stronghold of the Etruscan city Veii, was five miles north of Rome on the Tiber. According to Livy, it revolted twice with the help of Veii: first in 335 BCE and again in 326–325. Most modern historians accept the latter date and take the former to be a doublet (that is, a competing version of the battle that was later incorporated into the main tradition). Eutropius mentions only one revolt and gives it the considerably earlier date of 438 BCE.

137. **ut Fīdēnae sextō, Vēī octāvō decimō mīliāriō absint** – *result clause* (W 237–38, ER 361, LFA 92, LFNM 319–20, CLC 130, A&G §537.1). **Fīdēnae . . . Vēī** – The names of some cities are plural, such as *Bāiae, Coriolī, Fīdēnae, Pompēiī*, and *Veiī*.

> 138. **Coniūnxērunt sē hīs et Volscī** – The Volsci continued to plague the Romans throughout this and much of the next century.

hīs – *dative of indirect object: to these [people]* (also in line 154).

139. **Mam. Aemiliō dictātōre et L. Quīntiō Cincinnātō magistrō equitum** – *ablatives absolute.* Since classical Latin lacks the present participle of *sum, esse* (cf. the English word *being*), two nouns or a noun and an adjective in the ablative case can function as an *ablative absolute* (W 193–94, ER 349, LFA 33, LFNM 298–99, CLC 218, A&G §419a). **L. Quīntiō Cincinnātō** – the dictator from chapter XVII.

140. **victī** – perfect passive participle of *vincō, -ere.*

captae – perfect passive participle of *capiō, -ere.*

excīsae – perfect passive participle of *excīdō, -ere.*

Chapter XX

> 141. **Post vīgintī deinde annōs Vēientānī rebellāvērunt** – Veii had supported the revolts of Fidenae (traditionally in 335 and 326–325 BCE). Although Eutropius mentions only one revolt in the preceding chapter, he seems to be using the end of the second traditional revolt as the point of reference here.

142. **missus est** – perfect passive of *mittō, -ere;* the subject is *dictātor.*

> **Fūrius Camillus** – The Roman tradition portrays Camillus as the statesman par excellence. He defeats the Etruscans at Veii, remains

continued

> loyal to his city even after exile, recovers the Roman ransom from
> the Gauls, and rebuilds the city after the siege is lifted. The histor-
> ical Camillus did, in fact, conquer Veii and was instrumental in
> Rome's recovery after 390 BCE.

Fūrius Camillus – in apposition to *dictātor*.

vīcit – perfect of *vincō, -ere*.

143. **cīvitātem diū obsidēns cēpit** – *Cīvitātem* is the object of both the
present participle *obsidēns* and the verb *cēpit*: *besieging the city for a
long time, he captured [it]*. **cēpit** – perfect of *capiō, -ere*.

> **diū obsidēns** – According to tradition, the siege lasted for ten years
> (the same length as the siege of Troy). It ended only after Camillus
> forced his way into the citadel by digging a tunnel through solid
> rock. See the boxed text *The Romans Tunnel into Veii's Citadel and
> Interrupt a Sacrifice to Juno*, page 26.

antīquissimam . . . dītissimam – in apposition to *cīvitātem*.

144. **eam** – The antecedent is *cīvitātem [Vēientānōrum]*.

> **Faliscōs** – Eutropius may here be confusing the name of the inhab-
> itants (*Faliscī*) with the name of their city (*Faleriī*).

commōta est – perfect passive of *commoveō, -ēre;* the subject is *invidia*.

145. **quasi praedam male dīvīsisset** – *Quasi* plus the subjunctive is
sometimes used to show *ostensible or supposed cause* (A&G §540.2): *on
the grounds that he had divided the spoils unfairly*. **dīvīsisset** – pluperfect
subjunctive of *dīvidō, -ere*.

146. **cīvitāte** – *ablative of separation* (W 163, ER 348, LFA 214, A&G §400):
from the city.

147. **Gallī Senonēs** – According to Livy, the marauding bands of Celts that captured Rome were the Senones, who had recently come into Italy and established themselves on the northern Adriatic coast.

148. **secūtī** – perfect participle of the deponent verb *sequor, sequī*.

149. **dēfendī** – passive infinitive of *dēfendō, -ere*.

potuit – perfect of *possum, posse*.

quod cum diū obsēdissent et iam Rōmānī famē labōrārent – *cum clauses (circumstantial)* (W 255–56, ER 361, LFA 504, LFNM 260–61, CLC 73, A&G §546). The first verb is a pluperfect subjunctive (*had besieged*); the second is an imperfect subjunctive (*were suffering*). **quod cum** – *Quod* stands first in the clause because it is used here as *et id* (LFA 204, A&G §308f). **obsēdissent** – pluperfect subjunctive of *obsideō, -ēre*. **famē** – *ablative of means or instrument* (W 116–17, ER 346, LFA 20, LFNM 486, CLC 326–27, A&G §409).

150. **acceptō aurō** – *ablative absolute* (W 193–94, ER 348, LFA 33, LFNM 298–99, CLC 218, A&G §419). **acceptō** – perfect passive participle of *accipiō, -ere*.

nē Capitōlium obsidērent – *negative purpose clause* (W 229–30, ER 362, LFA 77, LFNM 40–41, CLC 221, A&G §531.1) after *acceptō aurō*.

151. **recessērunt** – perfect of *recēdō, -ere*.

152. **Gallīs superventum est** – Verbs that govern the dative in the active voice (e.g., **Gallīs** *supervēnērunt, they came upon the Gauls in surprise*) retain the dative when used impersonally in the passive voice (**Gallīs** *superventum est, it was come upon the Gauls in surprise = the Gauls were come upon in surprise*) (LFA 496, LFNM 503, A&G §372). **superventum est** – perfect passive of *superveniō, -īre*.

153. **victī sunt** – perfect passive of *vincō, -ere*.

secūtus eōs Camillus ita cecīdit ut et aurum . . . revocāret – The tradition that Camillus, who had been in exile, defeated the retreating

continued

Gauls and recaptured the city's ransom probably arose to restore
Roman honor. By placing him outside the city during the battle of
Allia, the story also relieves the hero of any culpability in the di-
saster.

secūtus eōs Camillus ita cecīdit – *Eōs* is governed by both the participle
secūtus and the verb *cecīdit: Camillus, having followed them, slaughtered
[them].* **secūtus** – perfect participle of the deponent verb *sequor, sequī.*
cecīdit – perfect of *caedō, -ere.*

154. **ut et aurum . . . et omnia . . . mīlitāria signa revocāret** – *result clause*
(W 237–38, ER 361, LFA 92, LFNM 319–20, CLC 130, A&G §537.1).
The verb *revocāret* governs two objects, *aurum* and *mīlitāria signa,*
each of which is modified by a relative clause.

mīlitāria signa revocāret – The loss of military standards in battle is
considered a great dishonor.

quod – The antecedent is *aurum.*

hīs – *dative of indirect object: to them* (i.e., the Gauls).

datum fuerat – pluperfect passive indicative of *dō, dare;* the auxiliaries
fuissem, fuissēs, etc., are sometimes used for *essem, essēs,* etc., in the
formation of the pluperfect passive (A&G §184, note).

cēperant – pluperfect of *capiō, -ere.*

155. **ingressus est** – perfect of the deponent verb *ingredior, -gredī.*

H. H. SCULLARD ON THE INDOMITABLE ROMAN SPIRIT

The city was destroyed; its internal stability was shaken; there was
no army of defense; the alliance with the Latins and Hernici had
collapsed; the Gauls might return. But in these dark days the spirit
of the Roman people did not waver. Wise leadership and the patri-

otism of the citizen body saved Rome. . . . So Rome set her shoul-
der to the grueling task of reconstruction at home and abroad; that
she accomplished so much is due largely to the wise direction of
Camillus.

A History of the Roman World: 753 to 146 BC, p. 95

VOCABULARY

All inflected forms used in Book I of the *Breviarium* are listed in square brackets at the end of the entries.

The following abbreviations are used in this section:

abl.	ablative
acc.	accusative
adj.	adjective
adv.	adverb
comp.	comparative
conj.	conjunction
demonstr. pron.	demonstrative pronoun
distrib. adj.	distributive adjective
f.	feminine
gen.	genitive
ind.	indicative
indecl.	indeclinable
indef. adj.	indefinite adjective
indef. pron.	indefinite pronoun
m.	masculine
n.	neuter
num.	numeral
part.	participle
pass.	passive
pl.	plural
prep.	preposition
pron.	pronoun
reflex. pron.	reflexive pronoun
relat.	relative
rel. pron.	relative pronoun

sing.   singular
subj.   subjunctive
subst.   substantive
sup.   superlative

A

ā, ab (*ā* only before consonants, *ab*
before vowels and some consonants),
prep. with abl., 1. in space, *from, away*
from, out of; 2. of time, *from, since,*
after; 3. to denote the agent, *by;* 4. to
denote source, origin, extraction,
from, of; 5. with verbs of freeing from,
defending, protecting, *from.*

absum, -esse, āfuī, -futūrum [ab + sum], *to*
be away from, be absent [absint, absunt].

ac (only appears before consonants)
conj., 1. in joining single words, *and,*
and even; 2. in connecting sentences
and clauses, *and indeed, and so.*

accēdō, -ere, -cessī, -cessum [ad + cēdō],
to go or come to or near, to approach, to
reach [accessit].

accipiō, -ere, -cēpī, -ceptum [ad + capiō],
to receive, get, accept, admit; to collect
[accēpit, acceptō].

aciēs, -ēī, f., *battle formation; battle [aciē].*

ad, prep. with acc., 1. in space, *to,*
toward; 2. in time, *about, toward;* 3. in
number or amount, *near, near to,*
almost, about, toward.

adeō, adv., *to such a degree.*

adhūc, adv. [ad + hūc], *until now,*
hitherto, as yet.

adiciō, -ere, -iēcī, -iectum [ad + iaciō], *to*
throw to or fling at, to add (by way of
increase) [adiēcit, adiectō].

adimō, -ere, -ēmī, -ēmptum [ad + emō],
to take away, take from, deprive of
[adēmit].

adiungō, -ere, -iūnxī, -iūnctum
[ad + iungō], *to fasten on, join to,*
harness [adiūnxit].

aedificō, -āre, -āvī, -ātum [aedis + faciō],
to build, erect a building [aedificāvit].

Aemilius, -ī, m., *Roman gens name.*
Mam. Aemilius Mamercinus, *dictator*
in 438 BCE who defeated the Fidenates,
Veientes, and Volsci (ch. XIX)
[Aemiliō].

aetās, aetātis, f., *the life of man, age,*
lifetime, years [aetātem].

ager, agrī, m., *field, farm, estate; territory,*
land [agrīs, agrōrum, agrum].

agō, -ere, ēgī, actum, *to act, do, perform,*
conduct; to spend, live [ageret, ēgerat,
ēgissent, ēgit].

Albānus, -a, -um, adj., *Alban;* as subst.,
Albānī, Albānōrum, *inhabitants of*
Alba Longa, an ancient Latin city just
south of Rome [Albānōs].

Algidus, -ī, m., *snow-capped mountain*
range southeast of Rome [Algidō].

aliquī, -qui, -quod, indef. adj. [alius + quī]
some, any [aliquā].

alius, -a, -ud, adj., *another, other, different*
[aliī].

Allia, -ae, f., *a stream that flows into*
the Tiber River near Rome, where the
Romans suffered a crushing defeat by the
Gauls in 390 BCE [Alliam].

alter, altera, alterum, adj., *another, the other [alter, alterō]*.

ambō, ambae, ambō, adj., *both (of a pair or couple) [ambae]*.

amīcus, -ī, m., *a loved one, loving one, friend [amīcīs]*.

ampliō, -āre, -āvī, -atum, *to widen, extend, increase, enlarge, amplify [ampliāvit]*.

ancilla, -ae, f., *a female attendant, handmaid [ancillā]*.

Ancus, -ī, m., *Ancus Marcius, the fourth king of Rome* (ch. V) *[Ancus, Ancī]*.

annus, -ī, m., *year [annīs, annō, annōs, annum, annus]*.

annuus, -a, -um [annus], adj., *for a year, lasting for a year [annuum]*.

Antemnātēs, -ium, m. pl., *inhabitants of Antemnae, an ancient Sabine town [Antemnātēs]*.

antīquissimus, -a, -um, adj. [sup. of antīquus], *very old [antīquissimam]*.

Ap., *abbreviation of the praenomen Appius*.

appellō, -āre, -āvī, -ātum [ad + pellō], *to address; to call by name, to name [appellātur, appellātus]*.

apud, prep. with acc., *at, near, by, with, among; of physical proximity, before, in the presence of*.

Ardea, -ae, f., *ancient port city of Latium [Ardeam]*.

ārdeō, -ēre, ārsī, ārsum, *to burn, be on fire [ārsit]*.

arō, -āre, -āvī, -ātum, *to plow, till [arāns]*.

Arrūns, -ūntis, m., *son of Tarquinius Superbus* (ch. X) *[Arrūns]*.

atque, conj., 1. *in joining single words, and, and even;* 2. *in connecting sentences and clauses, and indeed, and so*.

aurum, -ī, n., *gold [aurō, aurum]*.

autem, conj., *but, however, moreover*.

auxilium, -ī, n., *help, aid, assistance, support [auxilia, auxilium]*.

Aventīnus, -ī, m., *Aventine, one of the seven hills of Rome [Aventīnum]*.

B

bellum, -ī, n., *war, warfare [bella, bellīs, bellō, bellum]*.

bene, adv. [bonus], *well*.

Brūtus, -ī, m., *Roman family name*.
L. Junius Brūtus, *Roman aristocrat who expelled Tarquinius Superbus from Rome and became one of the first consuls* (chs. VIII–X) *[Brūtī, Brūtum, Brūtus]*.

C

C., *abbreviation of the praenomen Gaius (originally spelled Caius)*.

caedō, -ere, cecīdī, caesum, *to cut, cut to pieces; to kill, conquer, rout [caesīs, cecīdit]*.

Caelius, -ī, m., *Caelian, one of the seven hills of Rome [Caeliō]*.

Caenīnēnsēs, -ium, m., *inhabitants of Caenina, an ancient Sabine town [Caenīnēnsēs]*.

Camillus, -ī, m., *Roman family name*.
M. Fūrius Camillus, *Roman statesman and dictator who was hailed as a second founder of Rome* (ch. XX) *[Camillō, Camillus]*.

Campānia, -ae, f., *a region in western Italy, south of Latium [Campāniam]*.

capiō, -ere, cēpī, captum, *to take, get,
    seize, capture* [captae, cēperant, cēperat,
    cēpit].
Capitōlium, -ī, n., *Capitoline, one of the
    seven hills of Rome, where the temple of
    Jupiter Optimus Maximus was situated*
    [Capitōliō, Capitōlium].
captīvus, -a, -um, adj. [capiō], *captive*
    [captīvā].
captus, -a, -um, see *capiō*.
caput, -itis, n., *head* [capita].
Cassius, -ī, m., *Roman gens name*. **Sp.
    Cassius**, *the first master of the horse*
    (ch. XII) [Cassius].
causa, -ae, f., *cause, reason; pretext* [causā,
    causam].
cēnsus, -ūs, m., *census* [cēnsum, cēnsus].
centum, indecl. num., adj., *hundred*.
certāmen, -inis, n. [certō], *struggle, battle,
    engagement* [certāmen].
cessō, -āre, -āvī, -ātum, *to be inactive,
    loiter, delay; to come to an end, cease*
    [cessāvit, cessisset].
Cincinnātus, -ī, m., *Roman family name*.
    L. Quīntius Cincinnātus, *the name
    Eutropius gives for the Roman dictator
    who defeated the Aequi in the battle
    of Mons Algidus and then laid aside
    his power* (chs. XVII, XIX); *the usual
    spelling of his gens name is Quīnctius*
    [Cincinnātō, Cincinnātus].
cingō, -ere, cīnxī, cīnctum, *to encircle,
    surround* [cingunt].
circum, prep. with acc., *around, about,
    all around*.
circus, -ī, m., *an enclosure for athletic
    events, especially chariot races* [circum].
cīvīlis, -e, adj. [cīvis], *pertaining to a
    citizen; civil* [cīvīlēs].

cīvis, -is, m., *citizen* [cīvium].
cīvitās, -ātis, f. [cīvis], *state, community;
    city* [cīvitās, cīvitāte, cīvitātem, cīvitātēs,
    cīvitātī].
Claudius, -ī, m., *Roman gens name*. **Ap.
    Claudius**, *Roman decemvir* (ch. XVIII)
    [Claudius].
claudō, -ere, -sī, -sum, *to close, shut up,
    confine* [clausīs].
cloāca, -ae, f., *sewer, drain* [cloācās].
coepī, -isse, coeptum, defective verb, *to
    begin* [coepēre].
coerceō, -ēre, -cuī, -citus [con + arceō], *to
    shut in; to restrain, check* [coercēret].
Collātīnus, -ī, m., *Roman family name*.
    L. Tarquinius Collātīnus, *traditionally
    one of the first consuls of Rome*
    [Collātīnī, Collātīnō, Collātīnus].
collātus, see *cōnferō*.
collēga, -ae, m. [colligō], *colleague*
    [collēga, collēgam].
colligō, -ere, collēgī, collēctum
    [con + legō], *to collect, bring together*
    [collēctīs, collēgisset].
colō, -ere, -uī, cultum, *to cultivate; to
    inhabit; to worship* [colēbat].
commoveō, -ēre, -mōvī, -mōtum
    [con + moveō], *to move, rouse, excite*
    [commōta, commōtīs, commōvit].
commūnis, -e, adj., *common*
    [commūnem].
compāreō, -ēre, -uī, — [con + pāreō], *to
    appear, be visible* [compāruisset].
compleō, -ēre, -ēvi, -ētum [con + pleō], *to
    fill up, complete* [complētus].
concidō, -ere, -cidī, — [con + cadō], *to fall*
    [concidērunt].
concitō, -āre, -āvī, ātum [con + citō], *to
    rouse, stir up, incite* [concitāvit].

conditor, -is, m. [condō], *founder* [*conditor*].

condō, -ere, -idī, itum [con + dō], *to found, build* [*condidit, conditā*].

cōnferō, cōnferre, cōntulī, collātum [con + fero], *to collect; to take refuge* [*collātīs, contulit*].

cōnfundō, -ere, cōnfūdī, confūsum [con + fundō], *to pour together; to confuse* [*cōnfūsum*].

coniungō, -ere, -iūnxī, -iūnctum [con + iungō], *to join, join together, unite, ally* [*coniūnxērunt*].

cōnsecrō, -āre, -āvī, -ātum [con + sacrō], *consecrate* [*cōnsecrātus*].

cōnsenēscō, -ere, -nuī, — [con + senēscō], *to become or grow old* [*cōnsenuit*].

cōnsilium, -ī, n. [cōnsulō], *plan, advice* [*cōnsiliō*].

cōnspectus, -ūs, m. [cōnspiciō], *look, view, vision* [*cōnspectū*].

cōnstituō, -ere, -uī, -ūtum [con + statuō], *to set up, create, establish* (ch. III); *to found* (ch. I) [*cōnstituit*].

cōnsuētūdō, -inis, f. [cōnsuēscō], *custom* [*cōnsuētūdine*].

cōnsul, -ulis, m., *one of the two chief magistrates of the Roman Republic. They were elected annually, and the year was generally called by their names,* e.g., C. Fabiō et L. Virgīniō cōnsulibus [*cōnsul, cōnsulēs, cōnsulibus*].

cōnsulāris, -e, adj. [cōnsul], *of a consul, of consular rank* [*cōnsulāre*].

cōnsulātus, -ūs, m. [cōnsul], *consulship* [*cōnsulātus*].

contendō, -ere, -dī, -tum [con + tendō], *to hasten* [*contendit*].

contrā, 1. as prep. with acc., *against;* 2. as adv., *opposite; on the other hand*.

contulī, see *cōnferō*.

Coriolī, -ōrum, m. pl., *a Volscian town* [*Coriolōs*].

corrumpō, -ere, -rūpī, -ruptum [con + rumpō], *to ruin, corrupt* [*corrumpere*].

crēdō, -ere, -didī, -itum, *to trust, believe* [*crēditus*].

creō, -āre, -āvī, -ātum, *to create; to elect, appoint* [*creāta, creātī, creātus, creāvit*].

Crustumīnī, -ōrum, m. pl., *inhabitants of Crustumium, a Sabine town* [*Crustumīnōs*].

cuiusdam, see *quīdam*.

cum, conj., 1. of time, *when, while, whenever;* 2. of cause, *since;* 3. of concession, *although* [*cum, cumque*].

cum, prep. with abl., *with, together with*.

D

damnō, -āre, -āvī, -ātum, *to condemn* [*damnātī, damnātusque*].

dē, prep. with abl., *from, out of; concerning*.

dēbeō, -ēre, -uī, -itum, *to owe; ought (plus infinitive)* [*dēbērent*].

dēcēdō, -ere, -ssī, -ssum [dē + cēdō], *to go away, depart; to die* [*dēcessit*].

decem, indecl. num., adj., *ten*.

decemvir, -ī, m. [decem + vir], *one of a commission of ten men, a decemvir* [*decemvirī, decemvirīs, decemvirō*].

decimus, -a, -um, num., adj. [decem], *tenth* [*decimō, decimum*].

dēfendō, -ere, -dī, -sum, *to ward off, protect* [*dēfendī*].

dēfēnsōr, -is, m. [dēfendō], *defender* [*dēfēnsōrem, dēfēnsōrēs*].

dēferō, -ferre, -tulī, -lātus [dē + ferō], *to record, register* [*dēlātīs*].

deinde, adv. [dē + inde], *next, then*.

dēlātus, -a, -um, see *dēferō*.

dēprecātiō, -ōnis, f. [dē + precor], *begging off, entreaty* [*dēprecātiōne*].

dēscrībō, -ere, -psī, -ptum [dē + scrībō], *to fix; to assign* [*dēscrīpsit*].

dētergeō, -ēre, dētersī, dētersus [dē + tergeō], *to wipe off* [*dētersō*].

dētersus -a, -um, see *dētergeō*.

deus, -ī, m., *god* [*deōs*].

dictātor, -is, m. [dictō], *dictator, a magistrate with supreme power chosen during times of crisis* [*dictātor, dictātōre, dictātōrī*].

dictātūra, -ae, f. [dictātor], *dictatorship* [*dictātūra*].

diēs, -ēī, m., *day* [*diēs*].

dignitās, -tātis, f., *rank, office; dignity* [*dignitās*].

dīmicō, -āre, -āvī, -ātum, *to fight, contend* [*dīmicāvit*].

dītissimus, -a, -um, adj. [sup. of dīves], *very rich, richest* [*dītissimam*].

diū, adv., *for a long time*.

diūturnitās, -tātis, f. [diūturnus], *length of time, duration* [*diūturnitātem*].

dīvidō, -ere, -vīsī, -vīsum, *to divide* [*dīvīsisset*].

dō, dare, dedī, datum, *to give* [*datum*].

domus, -ūs or **-ī**, f., *home, house; family* [*domō*].

ducentī, -ae, a, num., adj., *two hundred* [*ducentīs*].

dūcō, -ere, dūxī, ductum, *to lead; to construct* [*dūcī, dūxit*].

duo, duae, duo, num., adj., *two* [*duo, duōbus, duōs*].

duodecimus, -a, -um, num., adj. [duo + decimus], *twelfth* [*duodecimō*].

duplicō, -āre, -āvī, -ātum [duplex], *to double* [*duplicāvit*].

dux, ducis, m. [dūcō], *commander, general, leader* [*ducēs, dux*].

E

eandem, see *īdem*.

ēdō, -ere, -didī, -ditum [ē + dō], *to bring forth; to give birth to* [*ēditus*].

ēgī, see *agō*.

ēiciō, -ere, ēiēcī, ēiectum [ē + iaciō], *to cast out; to expel* [*ēiectī*].

enim, conj., always postpositive, *namely, in fact, you know, for, because*.

eō, īre, iī, itum, *to go, come, march* [*euntibus*].

eōdem, see *īdem*.

eques, equitis, m. [equus], *horseman, knight*; **magister equitum**, *master of the horse, the Roman dictator's second-in-command* [*equitum*].

erant, erat, see *sum*.

ergō, adv., *therefore*.

Ēsquilīnus, -a, -um, adj., *of the Esquiline, one of the seven hills of Rome* [*Ēsquilīnum*].

esse, essent, esset, est, see *sum*.

et, conj., *and, also, even*; **et . . . et**, *both . . . and*.

etiam, conj. [et + iam], *also, even*.

euntibus, see *eō*.

ex, prep. with abl., 1. of place, *out of, from*; 2. of cause, *in consequence of, because of; according to*.

exāctus, -a, -um, see *exigō*.

excidium, -ī, m. [excīdō], *ruin, destruction* [*excidium*].

excīdō, -ere, -cīdī, -cīsum [ex + caedō], *to raze, demolish, destroy utterly* [*excīsae*].

exclūdō, -ere, -clūsī, -clūsum [ex + claudō], *to shut out* [*exclūsus*].

exercitus, -ūs, m. [exerceō], *army* [*exercitum, exercitus, exercituum*].

exigō, -ere, -ēgī, -āctum [ex + agō], *to drive out* [*exāctōs*].

exiguus, -a, -um [exigō], *small, slight* [*exiguam*].

exōrdium, -ī, n. [ex + ōrdō], *beginning;* exōrdium habere, *to derive one's origin* [*exōrdium*].

expellō, -ere, -pulī, -pulsum [ex + pellō], *to drive out, expel* [*expulsīs, expulsus*].

expulsus, -a, -um, see expellō.

exulō, -āre, -āvī, -ātum [exul], *to be in exile* [*exulābat*].

F

Fabius, -a, -um, adj., *Fabian, of the Fabii;* Fabius, -ī, m., *prominent Roman gens name.* C. Fabius (Vibulanus), *the name Eutropius gives for one of the consuls in 479 BCE, during the Cremera disaster (ch. XVI); Livy gives his praenomen as Caeso* [*Fabiā, Fabiō*].

faciō, -ere, fēcī, factum, *to make, do; to appoint* [*factī, factus, fēcerat, fēcit*].

Faliscī, -ōrum, m. pl., *inhabitants of the Etruscan city Falerii, conquered by Camillus during the war with Veii* [*Faliscōs*].

famēs, -is, f., *hunger, starvation* [*famē*].

familia, -ae, f., *family (as a branch of a gens)* [*familiā*].

fātāliter, adv. [fātālis], *by fate.*

fēcī, see faciō.

fēmina, -ae, f., *woman* [*fēminā, fēminam*].

ferē, adv., *almost, generally; nearly, approximately.*

fermē, adv., *almost, nearly.*

ferō, ferre, tulī, lātum, *to carry, bear, bring; to say, relate* [*ferente*].

Fīdēnae, -ārum, f. pl., *a town five miles north of Rome that was a stronghold of the Etruscan city Veii.*

Fīdēnātēs, -ium, m. pl., *inhabitants of Fidenae.*

fīlia, -ae, f., *daughter* [*fīliā, fīliae, fīliam*].

fīlius, -ī, m., *son* [*fīliī, fīliōs, fīlius*].

fīnitī, -ōrum, m. pl. [subst. of fīnitimus, from finis], *neighbors* [*fīnitimōrum*].

flētus, -ūs, m. [fleō], *weeping* [*flētū*].

flūmen, -minis, n., *river, stream* [*flūmen*].

fossa, -ae, f., *ditch, trench* [*fossās*].

frāter, -tris, m., *brother* [*frātre*].

fugiō, -ere, fūgī, —, *to flee, escape* [*fūgit*].

fuī, see sum.

fulmen, -minis, n., *thunderbolt* [*fulmine*].

Fūrius, -ī, m., *Roman gens name.*

M. Fūrius Camillus, *Roman statesman and dictator who was hailed as a second founder of Rome* (ch. XX) [*Fūrius*].

G

Gabiī, -ōrum, m. pl., *town near Rome* [*Gabiōs*].

Galus, -a, -um, adj., *Gallic;* as subst., Galī, -ōrum, m., *the Gauls* [*Gallī, Gallīs*].

gener, generī, m., *son-in-law* [*gener, generī*].

genitus, see gignō.

gēns, gentis, f., *race, family, clan* [*gēns, gentibus*].

gerō, -ere, gessī, gessum, *to wage, conduct* [*gessit*].

gessī, see *gerō.*

gignō, -ere, genuī, genitum, *to bear, give birth to* [*genitus*].

gravissimē, adv. [sup. of graviter], *most severely.*

H

habeō, -ēre, -uī, -itum, *to have, hold, possess, keep; to regard, consider* [*habēbant, habēbat, habēns, habērent, habet, habitus, habuerit, habuit*].

hic, haec, hoc, demonstr. adj. or pron., *this, these; he, she, it, they; the following* [*hāc, haec, hic, hīs, hunc*].

hinc, adv., 1. in space, *from here;* 2. of time, *from this point forward.*

homō, hominis, m. and f., *human being; man, mankind* [*hominēs*].

honestus, -a, -um, adj., *honorable, honest* [*honestīs*].

Horātius, -ī, m. *Roman gens name.* **Horātius Pulvillus,** *an early Roman consul (ch. X)* [*Horātium*].

Hostīlius, -ī, m., *Roman gens name.* **Tullus Hostīlius,** *the third king of Rome* (ch. IV) [*Hostīlius*].

hostis, -is, m., *enemy* [*hostibus*].

I

iam, adv., *now, already, at once.*

Iāniculum, -ī, n., *Janiculum, one of the seven hills of Rome* [*Iāniculum*].

ibi, adv., *there, in that place; then.*

īcō, -ere, īci, ictum, *to strike, hit* [*ictus*].

īdem, eadem, idem, demonstr. adj. or pron., *the same;* introducing a further attribute, *too, also, furthermore* [*eandemque, eōdem, īdem, īsdem*].

igitur, adv., *then, accordingly, therefore.*

ille, illa, illud, demonstr. adj. or pron., *that* [*ille*].

imperium, -ī, n. [imperō], *power or authority to rule; reign, rule; empire* [*imperiī, imperium*].

imperō, -āre, -āvī, -ātum, *to rule over, reign; to command* [*imperāsset, imperāvērunt*].

impleō, -ēre, -ēvī, -ētum [in + pleō], *to fill up, fulfill, carry through* [*implendum*].

in, prep. with acc., 1. of place, *into, to, on, upon, toward, against;* 2. in other relations, *against;* prep. with abl., 3. of place, *in, on, upon, in the midst of, among;* 4. of time, *in, in the course of, during.*

inchoō, -āre, -āvī, -ātum, *to begin, commence* [*inchoāvit*].

incognitus, -a, -um, adj. [in + cognōscō], *unknown* [*incognitus*].

īnferō, inferre, intulī, inlātum [in + ferō], *to bring something (acc.) into or against something else (dat.);* **bellum inferre,** *to make war on (plus dat.)* [*intulissent, intulit*].

īnfīnītus, -a, -um, adj. [in + finiō], *boundless, innumerable* [*īnfīnīta*].

ingēns, -entis, adj., *large, huge, great* [*ingentem*].

ingredior, -ī, -gressus sum [in + gredior], *to enter, begin* [*ingressus*].

ingressus, see *ingredior.*

iniūria, -ae, f. [in + iūs], *injury, insult; outrage* [*iniūriā, iniūriam*].

īnsolens, -entis, adj. [in + soleō], *insolent*
[*īnsolentiōrēs*].

īnstituō, -ere, -uī, -ūtum [in + statuō], *to
found, establish* [*īnstituit*].

inter, prep. with acc., *between, among.*

intrō, -āre, -āvī, -ātum, *to enter* [*intrāvit*].

intulī, see *īnferō.*

inveniō, -īre, -vēnī, -ventum [in + veniō],
to find, discover [*inventa, inventus*].

invidia, -ae, f., *jealousy, spite,
unpopularity* [*invidia*].

invītō, -āre, -āvī, -ātum, *to invite*
[*invītāvit*].

Iovis, see *Iuppiter.*

ipse, -a, -um, intensive pron. and adj.,
himself, herself, itself, themselves [*ipse,
ipsīque, ipsīus, ipsō, ipsōs*].

īrāscor, -ārī, īrātus sum [īra], *to become
angry* [*īrātus*].

īrātus, -a, -um, see *īrāscor.*

is, ea, id, demonstr. pron. and adj., *this,
that; he, she, it; such* [*eā, eam, eaque,
eārum, eī, eius, eō, eōs, eum, is*].

īsdem, see *īdem.*

ita, adv. [is], *in this way, so, thus; as
follows, in such a way; accordingly, and
so.*

Italia, -ae, f., *Italy* [*Italiaeque*].

itaque, adv. [ita + que], *and so, therefore,
consequently.*

iterum, adv., *again, a second time.*

iūdex, -icis, m. or f. [iūs + dicō], *judge*
[*iūdicēs*].

iūgerum, -ī, in pl. iūgera, -um, n.
[iungō], *an acre (roughly)* [*iūgerum*].

iungō, -ere, iūnxī, iūnctum, *to join, unite*
[*iūnxit*].

iūnior, adj. [comp. of iuvenis], *younger*
[*iūnior*].

Iūnius, -ī, m., *Roman gens name.*
L. Iūnius Brūtus, *Roman aristocrat
who expelled Tarquinius Superbus from
Rome and became one of the first consuls*
(chs. VIII–X) [*Iūnius*].

Iuppiter, Iovis, m., *Jupiter, the chief
Roman god* [*Iovis*].

K

Kal., *abbreviation of Kalendae, the
first day of the month in the Roman
calendar.*

L

L., *abbreviation of the praenomen Lucius.*

labōrō, -āre, -āvī, -ātum [labor], *to work;
to toil, suffer* [*labōrārent*].

Larcius, -ī, m., *Roman gens name.* **T.
Larcius,** *the first Roman dictator* (ch.
XII) [*Larcius*].

Latīnī, -ōrum, m. pl., *the Latins,
inhabitants of the plain of Latium
(modern-day Lazio)* [*Latīnōs*].

latrō, -ōnis, m., *bandit, robber* [*latrōnēs*].

latrōnicor, -ārī, -ātus sum [latrō], *to be or
live as a bandit* [*latrōcinārētur*].

lēgātus, -ī, m., *ambassador, envoy; deputy
officer* [*lēgātīs*].

legō, -ere, lēgī, lēctum, *to select; to read*
[*lēgit*].

lēx, lēgis, f., *law, condition (of a treaty)*
[*lēgēs*].

līberī, -ōrum, m. pl., *children* [*līberīs*].

līberō, -āre, -āvī, -ātum [līber], *to set free,
release* [*līberāvit*].

locus, -ī, m., *place* [*locō*].

longē, adv., *far; very far; very much.*

longius, adv. [comp. of *longē*], *farther.*

Lucrētia, -ae, f., *Roman matron, wife of Collatinus, whom Sextus Tarquinius raped* (ch. VIII) *[Lucrētiae, Lucrētiam].*

Lucrētius, -ī, m., *Roman gens name.*
Sp. Lucretius Tricipitinus, *Roman aristocrat, father of Lucretia* (ch. X) *[Lucrētium, Lucrētius].*

lūdus, -ī, m., *game, sport;* in pl., *public games [lūdōrum, lūdōs].*

lūgeō, -ēre, lūxī, lūctum, *to mourn, lament [lūxērunt].*

lūxī, see *lūgeō.*

M

magister, -trī, m., *master, chief, leader;* **magister equitum**, *master of the horse, the Roman dictator's second-in-command [magister, magistrō].*

magnus, -a, -um, adj., *great, large, abundant, powerful [magnōrum].*

māior, -is, adj. [comp. of *magnus*], *greater, larger, more powerful [maior].*

Maius, -a, -um, adj., *of the month of May [Maiās].*

male, adv. [*malus*], *badly, ill, unhappily, unsuccessfully.*

Mam., *abbreviation of the praenomen Mamercus.*

manus, -ūs, f., *hand, arm; band, troop [manibus].*

Mārcius, -ī, m., *Roman gens name.*
Q. Marcius Coriolanus, *the name Eutropius gives for the Roman general said to have laid siege to Corioli and later to have joined the Volsci against Rome* (ch. XV); *Livy gives his praenomen as Gnaeus [Mārcius].*

mare, -is, n., *sea [mare].*

marītus, -ī, m., *husband [marītō, marītus].*

Mārs, Mārtis, m., *Mars, the Roman god of war [Mārtis].*

māter, -tris, f., *mother [māter].*

mātrōna, -ae, f. [*māter*], *married woman, matron [mātrōnae].*

maximē, adv. [sup. of *magis*], *chiefly, most.*

memoria, -ae, f., *memory, remembrance; history, record [memoriam].*

mēnsis, -is, m., *month [mēnsēs].*

migrō, -āre, -āvī, -ātum, *to migrate, depart [migrāvit].*

mīles, mīlitis, m., *soldier [mīlitēs].*

mīlia, -um, num., n. pl., *thousand, thousands [mīlia].*

mīliārium, -ī, n. [*mīlia*], *milestone, mile [mīliāriō, mīliārium].*

mīlitāris, -e, adj. [*mīles*], *military; warlike [mīlitāria].*

mīlitō, -āre, -āvī, -ātum [*mīles*], *to serve as a soldier, perform military service; to make war [mīlitārat].*

minimus, -a, -um, adj. [sup. of *parvus*], *the smallest, very small [minimumque].*

minus, adv. [comp. of *parvē*], *less.*

missus, -a, -um, see *mittō.*

mittō, -ere, mīsī, missum, *to send, dispatch [missus].*

mōns, montis, m., *mountain, hill [monte, montem, montēs].*

morbus, -ī, m., *sickness, disease;* in abl., *by disease (as opposed to violence), by natural causes [morbō].*

morior, morī, mortuus sum, *to die;* as adj., **mortuus, -a, -um**, *dead [mortuō, mortuus].*

mōs, mōris, m., *custom, habit;* in pl.,
character, morals [mōrēsque].

moveō, -ēre, mōvī, mōtum, *to move; to
stir up [mōvit].*

mox, adv., *soon.*

multitūdō, -dinis, f. [multus], *a large
number, multitude, population
[multitūdinem].*

multus, -a, -um, adj., *much, many [multīs].*

mūrus, -ī, m., *wall [mūrōs, mūrum].*

N

nam, conj., *for, but.*

nāscor, -ī, nātus sum, *to be born; to spring
from, arise [nātus].*

nātiō, -ōnis, f. [nāscor], *tribe; people
[nātiōnēs].*

nē, conj., *in order that not, lest, not to.*

nepōs, nepōtis, m., *grandson, descendant
[nepōs].*

neque, conj., *and not, nor;* neque . . .
neque, *neither . . . nor.*

nisi, conj. [nē + sī], *unless, if not, except.*

nōbilis, -e, adj., *well-known, famous;
noble, highborn [nōbilem, nōbilēs,
nōbilī, nōbilissimam].*

nōmen, -inis, n., *name [nōmen, nōmine].*

nōminō, -āre, -āvī, -ātum [nōmen], *to
name, call [nōminātī, nōmināvit].*

nōn, adv., *not, no.*

nōnāgēsimus, -a, -um, num., adj.
[novem], *ninetieth [nōnāgēsimō].*

nōnus, -a, -um, num., adj. [novem],
ninth [nōnō].

noster, -tra, -trum, adj. [nōs], *our [nostram].*

novus, -a, -um, adj., *new; strange [nova].*

nūllus, -a, -um, adj. [ne + ūllus], *none, no
[nūllum].*

Numa, -ae, m., *Numa Pompilius, the
legendary second king of Rome* (ch.
III) *[Numa, Numae].*

numerus, -ī, m., *number [numerum].*

nummus, -ī, m., *a coin; money
[nummīs].*

O

ob, prep. with acc., *on account of.*

obsequor, -sequī, -secūtus sum
[ob + sequor], *to obey [obsequerētur].*

obsideō, -ēre, -sēdī, -sessum [ob + sedeō],
*to besiege [obsēdissent, obsidēns,
obsidērent, obsidērētur].*

occīdō, -ere, -cīdī, -cisum [ob + caedō], *to
kill, slay [occīdērunt, occīdit, occīsus].*

occupō, -āre, -āvī, -ātum [ob + capiō], *to
seize, occupy [occupāvērunt].*

octāvus, -a, -um, num., adj. [octō], *eighth
[octāvō].*

octō, indecl. num., adj., *eight.*

Olympias, -iadis, f., *an Olympiad, a
period of four years [Olympiadis].*

omnīnō, adv. [omnis], *at all, all together.*

omnis, -e, adj., *all, every [omne, omnēs,
omnī, omnia, omnibus, omnium].*

oppidum, -ī, n., *town [oppida].*

oppugnō, -āre, -āvī, -ātum [ob + pugnō],
*to storm, besiege [oppugnābat,
oppugnāns, oppugnātūrus].*

optimus, -a, -um, adj. [comp. of bonus],
best [optimam].

opus, -eris, n., *work [opere].*

orbis, -is, m., *circle; world [orbem].*

ōrdinō, -āre, -āvī, -ātum [ōrdō], *to
arrange; to carry out [ōrdināvit].*

orior, -īrī, ortus sum, *to arise; to begin; to
spring from [ortā].*

ōstium, -ī, n. [ōs], *mouth (of a river)* [*ōstium*].

P

paene, adv., *almost*

Palātīnus, -a, -um, adj., *of the Palatine, one of the seven hills of Rome* [*Palātīnō*].

parēns, -entis, m. or f. [pariō], *parent; relative* [*parēns*].

partus, -ūs, m. [pariō], *birth* [*partū*].

parum, adv., *too little; a small amount.*

pāstor, -ōris, m. [pāsco], *shepherd* [*pāstōrēs*].

pater, -tris, m., *father* [*pater, patrem, patrī*].

patria, -ae. f. [pater], *native country, fatherland* [*patriae, patriam*].

patrimōnium, -ī, n. [pater], *inheritance, patrimony; personal property* [*patrimōniō*].

pauper, -eris, adj., *poor* [*pauper*].

pāx, pācis, f., *peace* [*pācem*].

pellō, -ere, pepūlī, pulsum, *to drive, banish, rout* [*pellerētur*].

per, prep. with acc., 1. of place, *through, across, over, throughout;* 2. of time, *through, during;* 3. of means or agency, *by means of, by the agency of, through.*

perdō, -ere, -didī, -ditum [per + dō], *to lose* [*perdidērunt, perdidit*].

pereō, -īre, -iī, -itum [per + eō], *to perish, die* [*periit, perīsset*].

permaneō, -ēre, -mānsī, — [per + maneō], *to remain, endure* [*permanent*].

petō, -ere, petivī, petītum, *to seek; to attack* [*petēbant*].

placeō, -ēre, -cuī, -citum, *to please;* as impersonal verb (plus dat.), *to resolve, decree* [*placuerat, placuit*].

plēbs, plēbis, f., *plebs, common people* [*plēbis*].

plūrimum, adv. [sup. of multum], *most.*

Pōmētia, see *Suessa Pōmētia.*

Pompilius, -ī, m., *Numa Pompilius, the legendary second king of Rome* (ch. III) [*Pompilius*].

populus, -ī, m., *people* [*populō, populum, populus*].

Porsenna, -ae, m., *Lars Porsenna, an Etruscan king who besieged Rome in the earliest years of the Republic* [*Porsenna, Porsennā*].

porta, -ae, f., *gate* [*portīs*].

positus, -a, -um, adj. [pōnō], *situated* [*positam*].

possideō, -ēre, possēdī, possessum [sedeō], *to possess* [*possidēns, possidēret*].

possum, posse, potuī, — [potis + sum], *to be able, can (plus infinitive)* [*posset, potuerat, potuit*].

post, 1. as adv., *after, later, afterward;* 2. as prep. with acc., *after, behind.*

posteā, adv. [post + is], *afterward.*

postquam, adj. [post + quam], *after, when.*

potestās, -tātis, f. [possum], *power, authority* [*potestās, potestātem, potestātis*].

potuī, see *possum.*

praeda, -ae, f., *booty, plunder* [*praedam*].

praestō, -āre, -stitī, -stitum [prae + stō], *to offer, present* [*praestābant, praestāret*].

praetextus, -a, -um, adj. [prae + textō], *having an edge, embroidered;* **toga praetexta**, *a purple- or crimson-bordered toga worn by high-ranking magistrates* [*praetextam*].

premō, -ere, pressī, pressum, *to press; to oppress* [*premerētur*].

prīmus, -a, -um, adj. [sup. of prior],
first, foremost [prīmā, prīmō, prīmum,
prīmus, prīmusque].

prīscus, -ī, m., *ancient, old.* **L. Tarquinius**
Priscus, *the fifth king of Rome* (ch. VI)
[*Prīscus*].

prius, adv. [prior], *before, sooner; previously.*

prīvātus, ī, m., *private citizen [prīvātōs,*
prīvātus].

prō, prep. with abl., *for, instead of, in*
exchange for.

proelium, -ī, n., *battle [proeliō,*
proeliōrum].

proficīscor, -ī, -fectus sum
[prō + faciscor], *to set out, proceed*
[*profectī*].

prōfuī, see *prōsum*.

prōmittō, -ere, -mīsī, -missum
[prō + mittō], *to promise [prōmittentēs].*

proprius, -a, -um, adj., *special, one's own,*
peculiar [propriōs].

propter, prep. with acc., *on account of.*

prōsum, prōdesse, prōfuī, — [prō + sum],
to be useful (plus dat.); to benefit, profit
(plus dat.) [prōfuit].

Pūblicola, -ae, m., *Roman family name.*
L. Valerius Publicola, *the name*
Eutropius gives for the consul in the
early Republic who advocated on behalf
of the plebeian citizen body (ch. IX);
Livy gives his praenomen as Publius
[*Pūblicola*].

pudīcitia, -ae, f. [pudīcus], *chastity, honor*
[*pudīcitiae*].

pudīcus, -a, -um, adj., *pure, chaste,*
modest [pudīcissimam].

puerīlis, -e, adj. [puer], *boyish [puerīlem].*

pugna, -ae, f., *battle, fight [pugnā,*
pugnam].

Pulvillus, -ī, m., *Roman family name.*
Horātius Pulvillus, *an early Roman*
consul (ch. X) [*Pulvillum*].

putō, -āre, -āvī, -ātum, *to believe, think,*
consider [putābantur, putātus].

Q

Q., *abbreviation of the praenomen*
Quintus.

quadrāgēsimus, -a, -um, num., adj.
[quadrāgintā], *fortieth [quadrāgēsimō].*

quadrāgintā, indecl. num., adj.
[quattuor], *forty.*

quantum, adv., *as much as; how much;*
as.

quarter, adv. [quattuor], *four times.*

quārtus, -a, -um, num., adj. [quattuor],
fourth [quārtō].

quasi, adv. [qua + sī], *as if, as; on the*
grounds that.

quattuor, indecl. num., adj., *four.*

quattuordecim, indecl. num., adj.
[quattuor + decem], *fourteen.*

queror, -ī, questus sum, *to express grief,*
lament; to complain [questa].

questus, -a, -um, see *queror*.

quī, quae, quod, 1. as rel. pron., *who,*
which, what, that; 2. *in place of a conj.*
and demonstr. pron., and this, and
that [cuī, quae, quam, quārum, quem,
quī, quō, quod, quōrum, quōs].

quicquam, see *quisquam*.

quīdam, quaedam, quoddam, indef.
adj., *a certain [cuiusdam].*

quidem, adv., *indeed, at least.*

quīnī, -ae, -a, num., distrib. adj.
[quīnque], *five apiece, five each [quīnōs].*

quīnque, indecl. num., adj., *five.*

Quīntius, -ī, m., *alternate spelling of the Roman gens name Quīnctius.*
L. Quīn(c)tius Cincinnātus, *Roman dictator who defeated the Aequi in the battle of Mons Algidus and then laid aside his power* (chs. XVII, XIX) *[Quīntiō, Quīntius].*

quīntus, -a, -um, num., adj. [quīnque], *fifth [quīntō, quīntum].*

Quirīnālis, -e, adj., *of the Quirinal, one of the seven hills of Rome [Quirīnālem].*

quisquam, quaequam, quicquam, 1. as indef. pron., *anyone, anything;* 2. as indef. adj., *any [quicquam, quisquam].*

quoque, adv., *also, too.*

R

rapiō, -ere, rapuī, raptum, *to snatch, carry off, seize [raptārum, rapuit].*

raptus, -a, -um, see *rapiō.*

rapuī, see *rapiō.*

Rēa, -ae, *Rea Silvia, the legendary daughter of Numitor and mother of Romulus and Remus [Rēae Silviae].*

rebellō, -āre, -āvī, -ātum [re + bellō], *to resume a war; to revolt [rebellāvērunt].*

recēdō, -ere, -cessī, -cessum [re + cēdō], *to withdraw, retire [recessērunt].*

recēpī, see *recipiō.*

recessī, see *recēdō.*

recipiō, -ere, -cēpī, -ceptum [re + capiō], *to take back, receive; to bring back [recēpit, reciperētur].*

reddō, -ere, -didī, -ditum [re + dō], *to give back; to make, render, cause to turn out [redderentur].*

rēgnō, -āre, -āvī, -ātum [rēx], *to rule, reign [rēgnantibus, rēgnāsset, rēgnātum].*

rēgnum, -ī, n. [rēx], *kingdom; kingly power [rēgnī, rēgnum].*

regredior, -ī, regressus sum [re + gredior], *to return [regressus].*

regressus, -a, -um, see *regredior.*

relinquō, -ere, -līquī, -lictum [re + linquō], *to leave behind, desert, abandon [relīquit].*

relīquī, see *relinquō.*

remaneō, -ēre, -mansī, — [re + maneō], *to stay behind, remain [remanēret].*

removeō, -ēre, -mōvī, -mōtum [re + moveō], *to move away, remove [remōvit].*

Remus, -ī, m., *the legendary twin brother of Romulus* (ch. I) *[Remō].*

reparō, -āre, -āvī, -ātum [re + parō], *to repair, restore, renew [reparāvērunt, reparāvit].*

repudiō, -āre, -āvī, -ātum, *to scorn, reject [repudiātīs].*

restituō, -ere, -uī, -titum [re + statuō], *to restore, reestablish [restituī].*

revocō, -āre, -āvī, -ātum [re + vocō], *to recall; to withdraw [revocāret].*

rēx, rēgis, m., *king [rēge, rēgem, rēgēs, rēgibus, rēgis, rēgum, rēx].*

Rōma, -ae, f., *Rome [Rōmā, Rōmae, Rōmam].*

Rōmānus, -a, -um, adj., *Roman;* as subst., Rōmānī, -ōrum, m. pl., *the Romans [Rōmānī, Rōmānīs, Rōmānōrum, Rōmānōs, Rōmānum, Rōmānus].*

Rōmulus, -ī, m., *the legendary founder of Rome* (chs. I, II) *[Rōmulō, Rōmulus].*

S

Sabīnī, -ōrum, m. pl., *the Sabines, an Italic people who inhabited a region near Rome [Sabīnī, Sabīnōs].*

sacrum, -crī, n., *sacred rite, ceremony [sacra].*

saepe, adv., *often.*

scelus, -leris, n., *crime, guilt [scelere].*

sciō, -īre, -īvī, -ītum, *to know [scīrent].*

secundus, -a, -um, num., adj. [sequor], *second [secundō, secundus].*

secūtus, -a, -um, see *sequor.*

sed, conj., *but.*

sēditiō, -ōnis, f., *sedition, riot, uprising [sēditiōnem].*

sēmibarbarus, -a, -um, adj., *half barbarous, half civilized [sēmibarbarī].*

semper, adv., *always.*

senātor, -is, m. [senex], *senator [senātōrēs, senātōrum].*

senātus, -ūs, m. [senex], *senate [senātū, senātuī, senātum].*

senectūs, -tūtis, f. [senex], *old age [senectūtem].*

senior, -ōris, adj. [comp. of senex], *older, elder;* as subst., *elderly person, an elder [seniōribus].*

Senonēs, -ium, m. pl., *a Gallic people who established themselves on the Adriatic coast of Italy in the fourth century BCE [Senonēs].*

septem, indecl. num., adj., *seven.*

septimus, -a, -um, num., adj. [septem], *seventh [septimō, septimus].*

sepultūra, -ae, f. [sepeliō], *burial [sepultūrae].*

sequor, -ī, secūtus sum, *to follow [secūtī, secūtus, sequentī].*

Servius, -ī, m., *Roman praenomen.* **Servius Tullius**, *the sixth king of Rome* (ch. VII) *[Servius].*

sextus, -a, -um, num., adj. [sex], *sixth [sextae, sextō].*

sī, conj., *if.*

sīcutī, adv. [sīc + ut], *as, just as.*

signum, -ī, n., *a (military) standard [signa].*

Silvia, see *Rēa.*

similis, -e, adj., *like, resembling (plus dat.) [similem].*

sine, prep. with abl., *without.*

singulī, -ae, -a, distrib. adj., *each one of, every single one.*

socer, -erī, m., *father-in-law [socerī].*

sōlus, -a, -um, adj., *alone, only [sōlī].*

Sp., *abbreviation of the praenomen Spurius.*

spectāculum, -ī, n. [spectō], *show, sight, representation [spectāculum].*

statim, adv., *right away, immediately.*

stīpendium, -ī, n. [stips + pendō], *soldier's pay [stīpendiīs].*

stuprō, -āre, -āvī, -ātum [stuprum], *to violate; to have illicit sexual intercourse with [stuprāsset].*

stuprum, -ī, n., *dishonor; illicit sexual intercourse [stuprum].*

sub, 1. prep. with acc., *under, toward, until, after;* 2. with abl., *under, beneath, close to.*

subigō, -ere, -ēgī, -actum [sub + agō], *to conquer, subjugate, subdue [subēgit].*

subitō, adv. [subitus], *suddenly.*

sublātus, -a, -um, see *tollō.*

succēdō, -ere, -cessī, -cessum [sub + cēdō], *follow after, succeed [successerat, successit].*

sūdor, -is, m., *sweat [sūdōre].*

Suessa Pōmētia, -ae, f., *Latin city [Suessam Pōmētiam].*

suī (gen.), **sibi** (dat.), **sē** (acc. and abl.), reflex. pron., sing. and pl., *himself, herself, itself, themselves [sē, sibi].*

sum, esse, fuī, futūrum, *to be, exist; to have, possess (plus dat.) [erant, erat, esse, essent, esset, est, fuerat, fuērunt, fuisset, fuit, futūrōs, sunt].*

summus, -a, -um, adj. [sup. of superus], *highest [summam].*

sūmō, -ere, sūmpsī, sūmptum, *to take, assume, choose [sūmpsit].*

sūmptus, -ūs, m. [sūmō], *expense [sūmptum].*

superbus, -a, -um, adj., *proud, haughty, disdainful.* **L. Tarquinius Superbus**, *the seventh and final king of Rome, expelled by an aristocratic coup led by L. Junius Brutus* (chs. VIII–XI) *[Superbī, Superbus].*

superfuī, see *supersum.*

superō, -āre, -āvī, -ātum [super], *to overcome, defeat, conquer [superātus, superāvit].*

supersum, -esse, -fuī, — [super + sum], *to remain, survive [superfuit].*

superveniō, -īre, -vēnī, -ventum [super + veniō], *to come upon by surprise (plus dat.) [superventum].*

supputātiō, -ōnis, f. [sub + putō], *computation, calculation, reckoning [supputātiōne].*

suprā, prep. with acc., *beyond, above, over.*

suscipiō, -ere, -cēpī, susceptum [sub + capiō], *to take up, undertake; to receive [suscēpērunt, suscēpit, suscipī].*

sustineō, -ēre, sustinuī, sustentum [sub + teneō], *to support; to endure, undergo [sustinēret].*

suus, -a, -um, adj. [suī], *his own, her own, its own, their own; his, her, its, their [suā, suae, suam, suī, suīs, suō, suus].*

T

T., *abbreviation of the praenomen Titus.*

tam, adv., *so, so much.*

tamen, adv., *notwithstanding, yet, still, for all that, all the same, however, nevertheless.*

tamquam, adv., *as if, just as; on the grounds that.*

tantus, -a, -um, adj., *so much, so great [tantā].*

Tarquinius, -ī, m., *a gens name of Etruscan origin.* **L. Tarquinius Collātīnus**, *husband of Lucretia and one of Rome's first consuls, later expelled from Rome because of his gens name* (chs. VIII, IX); **L. Tarquinius Priscus**, *the fifth king of Rome* (ch. VI); **L. Tarquinius Superbus**, *the seventh and final king of Rome, expelled by an aristocratic coup led by L. Junius Brutus* (chs. VIII–XI) *[Tarquiniī, Tarquiniō, Tarquinium, Tarquinius].*

tempestās, -tātis, f. [tempus], *storm [tempestāte].*

templum, -ī, n., *temple [templa, templum].*

terra, -ae, f., *land, earth [terrārum].*

territōrium, -ī, n. [terra], *domain, territory [territōriō].*

tertius, -a, -um, num., adj. [trēs], *third;* **tertiō**, *as adv., for the third time [tertiō].*

Tiberis, -is, m., *the Tiber River, Rome's main waterway [Tiberis].*

toga, -ae, f., *toga, the outer garment worn by male Roman citizens [togam].*

tollō, -ere, sustulī, sublātum, *to take away [sublāta, sublātum].*

Tolumnius, -ī, m., *the king of the Veientes*

*who aided the Fidenates in their
rebellion against the Romans in the fifth
century BCE* (ch. XIX) *[Tolumnius].*

trādō, -ere, -didī, -ditum [trāns + dō], *to
hand down; to relate [trādunt].*

trānseō, trānsīre, trānsiī, trānsitum
[trāns + eō], *to cross over, pass through
[trānsīsse].*

trecentēsimus, -a, -um, num., adj.
[trēs + centum], *three hundredth
[trecentēsimō].*

trecentī, -ae, -a, num., adj.
[trēs + centum], *three hundred [trecentī].*

trēs, tria, num., adj., *three [trēs, tribus].*

tribūnus, -ī, m., *tribune, elected representative
of the plebeian order [tribūnōs].*

tribus, see *trēs*.

trīcēsimus, -a, -um, num., adj. [trēs],
thirtieth [trīcēsimō].

Tricipitīnus, -ī, m., *Roman family name.*
Sp. Lucretius Tricipitinus, *father of
Lucretia and early Roman consul* (ch.
X) *[Tricipitīnum].*

trīgintā, indecl. num., adj. [trēs], *thirty.*

triumphō, -āre, -āvī, -ātum, *to celebrate a
triumph [triumphāns, triumphātum].*

Trōia, -ae, f., *Troy, an ancient city in
Asia Minor from which came Aeneas,
the legendary ancestor of the Romans
[Trōiae].*

Tullius, -ī, m., *Roman gens name.* **Servius
Tullius**, *the sixth king of Rome* (ch. VII)
[Tullius].

Tullus, -ī, m., *archaic Roman praenomen.*
Tullus Hostilius, *the third king of Rome*
(ch. IV) *[Tullus].*

tum, adv., *then, at that time; thereupon.*

tumultus, -ūs, m., *uprising, rebellion;
tumult [tumultum].*

Tuscī, -ōrum, m. pl., *the Etruscans,
inhabitants of Etruria [Tuscīs].*

Tuscia, -ae, f., *alternative name for Etruria
(modern-day Tuscany), the region north
of Rome [Tusciae].*

Tusculum, -ī, *Etruscan town [Tusculum].*

tūtus, -a, -um, adj., *safe; protected [tūtus].*

U

ubi, adv., *when, where.*

ultimus, -a, -um, adj. [sup. of ulterior],
farthest, last, utmost, greatest [ultimus].

ūndecimus, -a, -um, num., adj.
[ūnus + decimus], *eleventh [ūndecimō].*

ūnus, -a, -um, adj., *one, only, sole, alone
[ūnō, ūnus].*

urbs, urbis, f., *city; the city of Rome [urbe,
urbem, urbī, urbis].*

usque, adv., *all the way, right on,
continuously, even.*

ut, conj., 1. with ind., *when;* 2. with subj.
of purpose, *in order that, that;* 3. with
subj. of result, *so that, that.*

uxor, -is, f., *wife [uxor, uxōre, uxōrem,
uxōrēs].*

V

Valerius, -ī, m., *Roman gens name.*
L. Valerius, *an early Roman consul*
(ch. XI) *[Valerius].*

Vēī, -ōrum, m. pl., *Veii, an Etruscan city
[Vēī].*

Vēientānī, -ōrum, m. pl., *inhabitants of
Veii [Vēientānī].*

Vēientes, -ium, m. pl., *inhabitants of Veii
[Vēientēs, Vēientium].*

veniō, -īre, vēnī, ventum, *to come,*

go, *approach* [vēnērunt, veniēnsque, vēnissent].

vērum, adv., *but, truly.*

Vestālis, -e, adj., *Vestal; of Vesta, the goddess of the hearth* [Vestālis].

Veturia, -ae, *the mother of the renowned general Q. Marcius Coriolanus* [Veturia].

vīcēsimus, -a, -um, num., adj. [vīgintī], *twentieth* [vīcēsimō].

vīcī, see *vincō.*

vīcīnus, -a, -um, adj., *near, neighboring* [vīcīnā, vīcīnae, vīcīnās].

vicis (gen.) [nom. sing. and gen. pl. not found], *change; turn;* **in vicem**, *in turn, alternately* [vicem].

victor, -ōris, m. [vincō], in apposition, *victorious* [victōrēs].

victus, -a, -um, see *vincō.*

vīgintī, indecl. num., adj., *twenty.*

Vīminālis, -e, adj., *of the Viminal, one of the seven hills of Rome* [Vīminālem].

vincō, -ere, vīcī, victum, *to conquer, defeat* [vīcit, victī, victōs, victus].

vindicō, -āre, -āvī, -ātum [vīs + dicō], *to avenge* [vindicandam].

Virgīnius, -ī, m., *alternate spelling of the Roman gens name Vergīnius.* **L. Virginius**, *the father of Verginia, the young woman whom the decemvir Appius Claudius attempted to rape* (ch. XVIII); **L. Virginius (Tricostus Rutilus)**, *the name Eutropius gives for one of the consuls in 479 BCE, during the Cremera disaster; Livy gives his praenomen as Titus* (ch. XVI) [Virgīniī, Virgīniō].

virgō, -inis, f., *maiden, virgin* [virginem, virginēs, virginis].

vix, adv., *scarcely, with difficulty.*

vocō, -āre, -āvī, -ātum [vōx], *to call, summon* [vocārētur, vocāvit].

volō, velle, voluī, —, *to wish, want; to be willing; to be inclined to, be disposed to* [voluisset, voluit].

Volscī, -ōrum, m. pl., *an Italic people who inhabited southern Latium and were one of Rome's principal threats in the region* [Volscī, Volscōrum, Volscōs].

Volumnia, -ae, f., *the wife of Coriolanus* [Volumnia].

Appendix A: Maps

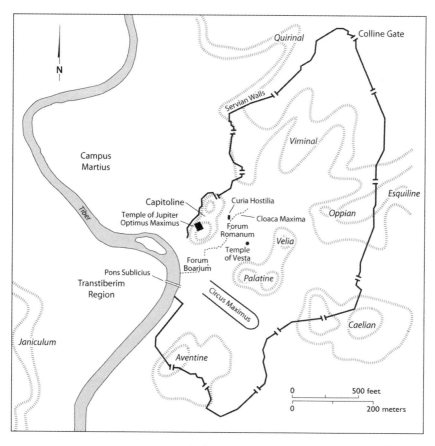

Early Rome

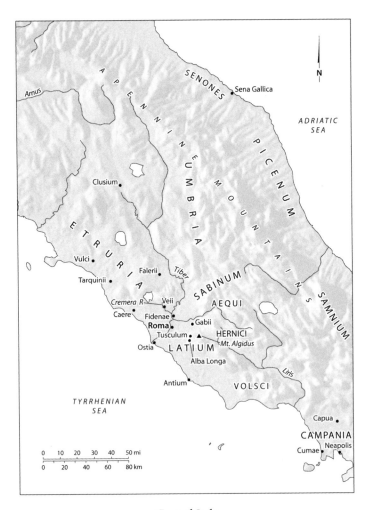

Central Italy

APPENDIX B: ADDITIONAL TEXTBOOK CROSS-REFERENCES

This appendix contains cross-references to the following textbooks not included in the parenthetical citations in the Commentary.

Abbreviations

J   *Jenney's Second Year Latin* (Upper Saddle River, NJ: Prentice Hall, 1990).

LTRL   *Learn to Read Latin*, by Andrew Keller and Stephanie Russell (New Haven: Yale University Press, 2003).

M&F   *Latin: An Intensive Course*, by Floyd L. Moreland and Rita M. Fleischer (Berkeley: University of California Press, 1977).

OLC   *Oxford Latin Course, Part III*, 2nd Edition (New York: Oxford University Press, 1997).

Selected Grammatical Constructions

ablative absolute: J 29, LTRL 226, M&F 162, OLC 138–39
ablative of cause: J 42, LTRL 110, M&F 164
ablative of manner: J 422, LTRL 58, M&F 50
ablative of means or instrument: J 420, LTRL 17, M&F 50
ablative of place where: J 42, LTRL 111, M&F 377
ablative of separation: J 419, LTRL 110, M&F 102
ablative of time when: J 422, LTRL 159, M&F 116
accusative of duration of time: J 418, LTRL 158, M&F 116

accusative of place to which: J 418, LTRL 112, M&F 372

apposition: J 413, LTRL 59, M&F 363

cardinal number with ex or *de:* J 420, M&F 154

connecting relative: LTRL 192, M&F 115, OLC 163–64

cum clause (adversative): J 213, LTRL 327–28, M&F 249, OLC 162

cum clause (causal): J 213, LTRL 327–28, M&F 248, OLC 162

cum clause (circumstantial): J 213, LTRL 327–28, M&F 248, OLC 161

dative with adjective: J 417, M&F 368

dative with the compound verb: J 41, LTRL 330, M&F 220

dative of separation: J 416

gerundive with *ad* or *causā:* J 42, LTRL 369, M&F 266, OLC 170

impersonal passive: J 203, LTRL 112, M&F 219, OLC 168

indirect statement: J 139, LTRL 272, M&F 100, OLC 148–50

jussive noun clauses (indirect command): J 78, LTRL 188, M&F 52,
    OLC 131

locative: J 423, LTRL 111, M&F 103

objective genitive: J 41, LTRL 72, M&F 178

partitive genitive: J 414, LTRL 71, M&F 154

personal agent expressed by *per:* J 419

predicate accusative: J 418, LTRL 273, M&F 101–2

predicate nominative: J 413, M&F 26, LTRL 15

purpose clause: J 68, LTRL 185, M&F 50, OLC 128

purpose clause introduced by the relative pronoun: J 227, LTRL 218,
    M&F 236, OLC 177

relative clause of characteristic: J 225, LTRL 219, M&F 234

result clause: J 106–7, LTRL 423, M&F 232, OLC 153–54

substantive: J 424, LTRL 52, M&F 10

BIBLIOGRAPHY

Annotated Editions

Beyer, Brian. *War with Hannibal: Authentic Latin Prose for the Beginning Student.* New Haven: Yale University Press, 2009.

Caldecott, W., ed. *Eutropius, Books 1, 2, with Notes and Vocabulary.* London: Longmans, Green, 1893.

Clark, Victor S., ed. *Eutropii Historia Romana: Selections from the History of the Republican Period.* Boston: Leach, Shewell, and Sanborn, 1897.

Clarke, John, ed. *Eutropii Historiæ Romanæ Breviarium with Notes, Critical, Geographical, and Explanatory, in English.* Dublin: J. Exshaw, 1815.

Greenough, J. B., ed. *Extracts from Eutropius.* Boston: Ginn, 1893.

Hamilton, James, ed. *Abridgment of the Roman History: With an Analytical and Interlineal Translation.* C. F. Hodgson and Sons, 1849.

Hazzard, J. C., ed. *Eutropius.* New York: American Book Co., 1898.

Jones, W. H. S., ed. *Eutropii Breviarium.* Blackie's Latin Texts. London: Blackie, 1905.

Laming, W. Cecil, ed. *Eutropius, Books I and II.* London and Glasgow: Blackie and Son, 1904.

Masters, Kristin A. *The First Twenty Roman Emperors: Selections from Eutropius Adapted for Beginning Readers of Latin.* Hamilton, OH: American Classical League, 2012.

Welch, W., and C. G. Duffield, eds. *Eutropius Adapted for the Use of Beginners with Notes, Exercises, and Vocabularies.* London: Macmillan, 1883.

White, John T., ed. *I–IV Books of Eutropius.* White's Grammar School Texts. London: Longmans, Green, 1887.

Critical Editions

Droysen, Hans, ed. *Eutropi Breviarium ab Urbe Condita cum Versionibus Graecis et Pauli Landolfique Additamentis.* Monumenta Germaniae Historica: Auctorum Antiquissimorum. Berlin: Weidman, 1879.

Rühl, Franz, ed. *Eutropi Breviarium ab Urbe Condita.* Bibliotheca Scriptorum Graecorum et Romanorum Teubneriana. Stuttgart: Teubner, 1887.

Santini, Carlo, ed. *Eutropii Breviarium ab Urbe Condita.* Bibliotheca Scriptorum Graecorum et Romanorum Teubneriana. Stuttgart: Teubner, 1979.

Wagener, C., ed. *Eutropi Breviarium ab Urbe Condita.* Bibliotheca Scriptorum Graecorum et Romanorum. Leipzig: G. Freytag, 1884.

English Translations

Bird, H. W., trans. *The Breviarium ab Urbe Condita of Eutropius.* Translated Texts for Historians 14. Liverpool: Liverpool University Press, 1993.

Erickson, Daniel Nathan. "Eutropius' Compendium of Roman History: Introduction, Translation, and Notes." PhD diss., Syracuse University, 1990.

Watson, J. S., trans. *Eutropius's Abridgment of Roman History.* London: G. Bell, 1853.

Lexicon

Segoloni, Maria Paola, and Anna R. Corsini, eds. *Eutropii Lexicon.* Perugia: Studium Generale Civitatis Perusii, 1982.

Online Versions

Corpus Scriptorum Latinorum. This site provides the complete Latin text of the *Breviarium* (from the 1887 Teubner edition) and the English translation and notes by J. S. Watson, hyperlinked to each other by chapter. www.forumromanum.org/literature/eutropius.

The Latin Library. This site provides the complete Latin text of the *Breviarium* from the 1887 Teubner edition. www.thelatinlibrary.com/eutropius.html.

Monumenta Germaniae Historica Digital. This database provides image files of the complete Droysen edition of the *Breviarium* (which includes the Greek version on facing pages, as well as the continuations of Paulus Diaconus and Landolfus Sagax). The images files include the preface, Greek and Latin text, critical apparatus, appendices, and indices. Main page: www.dmgh.de. Eutropius files: http://mdz1.bib-bvb.de/~db/bsb00000787/images/index.html.

INDEX OF SELECTED GRAMMATICAL CONSTRUCTIONS

All numerical references are to line numbers.